Enjoy these with
my love

I REMEMBER
Pasta

A Celebration of Food, Family and Friends

by

Carol Lawrence

Harvest House Publishers
Eugene, OR 97402

I REMEMBER PASTA

Copyright © 1996 by Carol Lawrence
Published by Harvest House Publishers
Eugene, Oregon 97402

Library of Congress Cataloging-in-Publication Data

Lawrence, Carol, 1937-
    I remember pasta / Carol Lawrence.
            p.   cm.
    ISBN 1-56507-363-0 (alk. paper)
    1. Cookery, Italian. 2. Lawrence, Carol, 1937-   . I. Title.
    TX723.L36   1996
    641.5945--dc20   96-11130
                                                            CIP

Design and production by Garborg Design Works, Minneapolis, Minnesota

Harvest House Publishers has made every effort to trace the ownership of all quotes and lyrics in this book. In the event of any question arising from the use of any quote or lyric, we regret any error made and will be pleased to make the necessary correction in future editions of this book.

96 97 98 99 00 01 02 03 04 05 / DR / 10 9 8 7 6 5 4 3 2

Acknowledgments

My dedication spotlights my deep gratitude to my
mother as my source of culinary treasures, but I
would be remiss if I didn't acknowledge the loving
network of relatives and friends who helped birth
this new entity, **I Remember Pasta**.

My adorable Aunt Ange confirmed and clarified many
of the easily forgotten tips (Mom never noted and
barely mentioned to me) that firmed up and made
manageable so many treats.
"Mille Grazie, Zia!"

I also thank my ever-patient brother, Joey,
and sweet sister-in-law, Mary Lou, who dug through
old chests for pictures and through their memories of
delectable dinners to help me put on paper what
was ever guarded.

I deeply appreciate my sons, Chris and Mike, for
chopping and mixing and trying and reworking
recipes so that they'd taste just like Nana's did.

And especially lifesaving was the encouragement,
organizational skills, brainstorming, and endless
support through the long months of accumulating
and eliminating wheat from the chaff by my dear
friend, Dr. Robin Woods.

I would have given up without these angels in my
life, and I thank the Lord for each one.

Contents

PART II:
I Remember Special People and Occasions

Mama and me on a
spring Sunday

Chapter 1

"Something's Coming"
The Loving Kitchen

*Something's comin',
I don't
know what
it is, but it is
gonna be
great...*

—WEST SIDE STORY

THE REAL JOY OF COOKING IS A THEATRICALLY REWARDING one. I have been a ham all my life, spending most of my childhood stretching and pushing my body to do things the Good Lord never intended it to do. It was part of studying the craft of setting a stage for an exciting finale that brings an audience cheering to its feet. As a child, I watched my mother do exactly that every time she set her table for company, and most times when she set it just for her family. That is the basic premise of this book—the similarity of enjoyment derived from a *set* on a theatre stage and a *place setting* on a dinner table. It's your creativity that determines either one's success. Let me explain.

I grew up in a small "village" called Melrose Park, some 22 miles west of Chicago. It seems only fair to explain that among the predominately Italian population of 20,000, there had to be at least 12,000 fantastic, gourmet, authentic, natural, genius cooks in residence (and don't contest any Italian Mama's talent in a kitchen if she has sons). But without exaggeration, I can tell you that my mother was the uncontested "Queen of Cuisine." People literally fasted for days before coming to break bread with Rosie Laraia and her family ("Laraia" is my real name).

Mom, Dad, Joey and me one Easter

Like every gourmet cook, Mama guarded her recipes and endless secret touches with cunning charm, leaving out a seemingly insignificant essential that reduced a heavenly taste to something you'd eat in purgatory. When someone would whine, "But Rosie, my angel food cake just wasn't as high and light as yours!" she'd reply with smiling concern, "Oh, honey. Your oven was too hot." It was fun to watch the game.

Since I was her only daughter, the authentic culinary delights were part of my inheritance and, until now, have remained a cherished and unshared treasure. Even as I write this, my two sons (who are half-Italian, after all) do not really approve of my divulging "Nana's specialties." When I asked my mother if she'd help me write this cookbook, she smiled that glowing smile and acquiesced, even though she was already ill. I have her precious handwritten love letters and from them I have compiled this book.

Here is a page from her own spiral notebook, with a typical recipe:

The water spots are the natural casualties of any cookbook on the nearby counter of a flamboyant Italian cook—and Mama created the role!

Savoring these unique concoctions excites all the human senses with each bite—from the visual beauty and aroma, to the texture, crunch, palate, and obvious nurturing care that went into them. The memory of the moment lingers in your very being longer than mere words can endure.

Of course, I'd be totally remiss (and a downright liar) if I told you I always ate the kind of rich and fattening food Mama promoted. I could never have gotten into a leotard, let alone faced an audition, weighing 200-plus pounds. So I somehow fought her off and left home for the Great White Way in my teens. I was lucky enough to support myself doing what I would have paid the producers to let me do—perform!

Inevitably, though, the hunger in my heart for authentic Italian "soul food" would win out, and I'd reconstruct a dish or two for special friends who would never stop pestering me to write a cookbook.

This book is really a loving, grateful tribute to a woman who nurtured me with encouragement, faith, support, hope, and boundless enthusiasm. And tucked inside that package was a delicious morsel called "food," which translated as "love" every time. I'd be happy if I could keep the zest for life flowing as it did whenever Mama was creating in the kitchen. No one could resist watching and helping and tasting and laughing with her. It's a tradition worth saving.

My proud Italian heritage claims the right to feed anyone who enters an Italian home. It's the Italian way to say, "Welcome! How are you doing? Thanks for helping me." And most of all, "I love you."

Since my cooking has been shared with countless casts and celebrities—Bing Crosby, Frank Sinatra, Red Skelton, George Burns, Bob Hope, Leonard Bernstein, and Mickey Rooney—you'll find anecdotes and pictures of them included with their favorite dishes. This book would also be incomplete without tidbits about friends and family and the bonding that keeps the kitchen the heart of my home.

I'd love you to accept this book as an ongoing script—a work in progress that brings an exciting theatrical flare to the daily drama called living!

THE LOVING KITCHEN

The kitchen is really the heart of the home. Energy and physical strength flow from this spot with a rhythm that reflects its host. As a child, it was the first place I learned my needs would be met with a drink of water, a piece of bread, or comfort and balm for a scraped knee. It was also where something was usually simmering into a delicious gift of caring.

Actually, my first cognizant awareness of food, fun, and hospitality came from my grandmother. Her Italian title was "Nana," and she was a pied piper of children with never less than eight grandchildren in her daily babysitting regime. I remember Nana attached great responsibility to washing her house-cleaning cloths on a washboard in a pot of soapsuds in her sink. She stood you on a chair to reach the sink and wrapped an enormous dish towel around your chest to keep you from getting soaked. She was a genius in getting you to do anything she suggested!

(left to right) My dad's mother, Grandma Laraia; my nana in her eighties; my Aunt Ange

She kept a zing in any operation by improvising a nonsense syllable (but rhythmically contagious) song to keep the rags zipping up and down the corrugated tin washboard. "Zing-a-zang-a-bottleley-boomaboom!" she'd sing liltingly and demonstrate until you *had* to grab the rag yourself—it looked so enticing!

The same ingenuity went into how she enlisted your creative imagination to conjure up your own idea of a gingerbread man or an "Angela" or "Dolly" (out of a piece of her freshly made bread dough). She'd sculpt her own little round man and press her fingers in the body to fill it with a raisin or nut. You would render your own design—with hat or scarf or shoes or belt of dough. At each of your own additions she'd clap and laugh and cheer and fuss over you. It felt marvelous—especially since she never made you wash your hands before fashioning your masterpiece! Since we loved climbing the apple trees or digging in the backyard, our gingerbread men popped out of the oven always grey in color as opposed to the spanking brightness of Nana's creations. But it tasted glorious 'cause it was all ours!

Maybe washing rags or making gingerbread men is not a part of our routine these days—but we can create lasting memories tied to whipping up immediately gratifying taste treats.

That's what I've tried to create in my own cooking haven. I've really been through a slew of kitchens in my life—from a tiny Pullman in a New York studio apartment to an antiquated nook in a fifth-floor walkup. I've even borrowed a restaurant kitchen for a cast party! But, in every one of these Heinz 57 varieties, the one common denominator was that my kitchen was warm, working, and open to all I love. So come on in. Things are starting to get cold!

How about your kitchen? Is it a haven? Is it ready to welcome those you love? I'm sure you already have the basics for a functional, loving kitchen. And while it isn't necessary to be extravagant when you buy cooking equipment, don't waste your money on flimsy items either. Purchase a reputable oversized skillet, two sturdy saucepans, and a steam basket rather than a collection of pieces you'll never use.

I'd like to recommend you have a few "luxury" items on hand, to make cooking from this book more enjoyable. (And if you don't have a certain piece of equipment, don't let it stop you! Improvise!)

> *large garlic press*
>
> *cheese grater with*
> *a variety of openings*
>
> *restaurant-sized skillet*
>
> *restaurant-sized stock pot*
>
> *food processor*

THE ART OF CREATING THE SHOW

I think as a performer; and I equate the necessary steps of preparing a meal to the steps of putting on a show. It would seem that everyone wants to be in show business anyway, so why not incorporate the two? Shakespeare was right: All the world's a stage. Let's begin with step one: Preproduction. Now you'll become a "producer" in your own kitchen!

Part of being a producer is developing a style that's uniquely yours. It will be what sets the tone for every meal you prepare. I think you'll find my style pretty lavish—just like my signature.

That signature has remained pretty much the same since I was 13 years old. For me, it was a brand new name and identity I was putting on, like a brightly sequined cloak. It was my professional name, chosen by my serious, patriarchal Italian father to replace the beautifully phonetic, but impossible to grasp quickly, original family name of "Laraia" (sounds like "Mariah" with an "L").

I was embarking on a professional adventure as a solo performer with my own act, to be part of my summer schedule when school was out. It was an order from Edna MacRae (my mentor and dance teacher), who insisted the only honest reading of your talents comes from a paying audience. I loved the job so much that summer that I decided "live" entertainment was where I had to be!

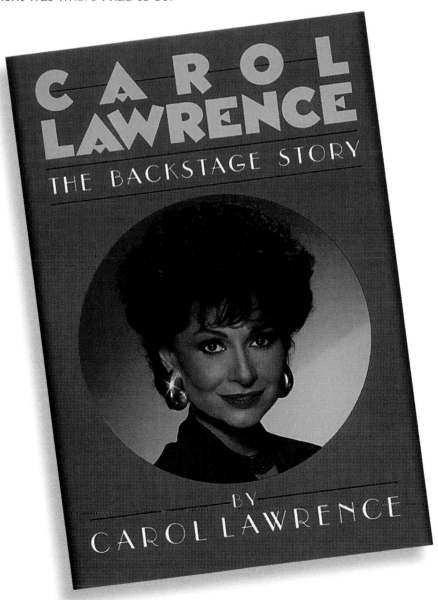

"Live" is the core of real entertaining, and *wherever* you are, doing something live gives you a signature, a style. Your signature needs to be as distinctive as your own personality. As a 13-year-old, I created an act to showcase my talents, picking songs, dances, and antics that presented my joyful message. In the same way, a meal in your home sets a stage for your gifts to be showcased and shared by those dear to you.

What will your signature be? What new treasures do you have to introduce? How can meals in your home be a truly personal expression of your love?

Life is a stage, and all the drama, pace, humor, music, and applause are yours to grasp! Every meal you prepare can be a cherished memory, signed in your favorite color and in your own style. Here's a line for your signature:

My recital picture when I was around 10 ("on pointe" for the first time)

Great! You're on your way!

Johnny Mercer, Rosemary Clooney, Bing Crosby, and Me. Because of the impact and success of <u>West Side Story</u>, I was privileged to be in countless musical TV specials such as this one. I had the honor of working with giants in show business.

Chapter 2

"Oh, What a Beautiful Morning!"
In the Beginning Is Breakfast

Oh, what a
beautiful
morning,
Oh, what a
beautiful day!
I've got a
beautiful feeling,
Everything's
going my way!

—OKLAHOMA

AS A DANCER ON TELEVISION, I HAVE ALWAYS HAD TO
compensate for the extra ten pounds the camera adds to your body on screen. To stay
ten pounds under your normal weight makes skipping breakfast an easy option. But in
the hectic schedules and stresses of today's work, that is a *big* mistake. So starting the
day right with a healthy breakfast has become a fact of my existence. I take lots of
powerful vitamins, and my stomach needs food right away to help these vitamins digest
and work well. In addition, the meal that starts the day is the easiest to burn away.

Have you noticed that breakfast has become one of those "keep in touch"
times? People with busy schedules often try to start their days by having breakfast with
someone they care about. Unfortunately, some people are just not "morning people,"
and the whole idea backfires on you.

Such was the sorry truth about Bing Crosby's warm-hearted breakfast invita-
tion to the cast of one of his marvelous TV specials. The cast consisted of just two
lucky people—Dean Martin and me. It was the first day of rehearsal at NBC in
Burbank, in Studio A. The call was for nine in the morning, and at ten minutes to, I
walked in, dressed to sing and dance. To my amazement, Bing cordially greeted me at
the door and escorted me to an extravagant buffet of breakfast elegance. It was more
food than three people could eat in a week—everything from hot scrambled eggs,
sausage, bacon, grapefruit, fresh strawberries and cream, bagels and lox with cream
cheese, sweet rolls, cereal and bananas, coffee, tea, and milk.

"What can I get for you, honey?" he crooned.

"Maybe a few strawberries, Bing, please." I couldn't stop staring at the spread.

We made small talk while we waited for Dino to arrive. Twenty minutes turned into 45 and finally the door opened again.

There Dino stood in a crumpled trench coat, leaning against the doorjamb, his sleepy eyes adjusting to the bright studio lights. "Whose idea was it to attempt singing at this hour, anyway?" he drolled.

Bing smiled and took the pipe out of his mouth. "I guess I'm to blame, Dino. I *love* to sing early in the day—just got used to it—all those years on the radio. Come in. What'll you have?"

"A scotch and water."

Bing blinked and said, "Well, Dino, we don't *have* any liquor, but we've lots of —."

"Okay, then," Dino interrupted, "I'll just have scotch."

It was an old vaudeville punchline, but we all laughed anyway.

Bing Crosby or not, if you're planning on a breakfast extravaganza a warning to your guest of honor is a wise choice. To this day neither of my sons can down anything until they've been up and dressed and acclimated to the beginning of a new day. Test the water before you start boiling it!

Breakfast can also be a time of reminiscing. At the holidays, relatives come "home," and breakfast is a great opportunity for creating new memories by recalling cherished old ones—especially if there is a favorite cereal or a muffin grandma used to make. One morning, when you have houseguests (without giving away the surprise), call them to sit down at a table set with old china, some favorite family heirlooms, and the aroma of freshly baked, almost-forgotten treats. This says that you cherish the "long ago time" enough to bring it to immediate life for new loved ones to carry on the tradition.

One such sensory memory can instantly make me feel six years old—the fragrance of my Aunt Teresa's poppyseed jelly-roll breakfast cake. Maybe because I'd never seen a food that was so black-and-white before or known about jelly-roll pastry, but this feat of magic made my aunt a kind of wizard to me. All these years it has remained a mysterious recipe because my mom never made it.

"Dino"
Martin
and me

Just a few months ago I asked my sweet Aunt Teresa what her secret was. She is almost blind now, but in her typical, quiet manner she said, "Why, it's merely a sweet dough, rolled out and spread with a poppyseed mix you can buy at any supermarket. Sorry honey, it's no more than that."

"Oh, Aunt Tree," I protested, "you're wrong. It will always be my most favorite sweet taste of love, when I remember being six in your loving kitchen for breakfast."

Have some fun with breakfast! Here are a few suggestions for things to do, along with some of my favorite ideas and anecdotes.

A SURPRISE BREAKFAST FOR YOUR OWN ROYALTY OF THE DAY

Have a surprise breakfast for a king or queen. Begin the preparations early and quietly enough to stun your favorite person and also to leave him or her time to savor your unexpected surprise. If the king or queen has a favorite dish, by all means make it! But just for fun, try fashioning a cardboard crown and scepter and cover them with aluminum foil. Place on a tray with a bud vase with a blood-red rose and the delectable breakfast items listed here.

The royal secret for putting your highness at ease is to awaken him or her with a tinkling bell and pop a mint candy in the person's mouth, eliminating the embarrassment of morning breath. A real lifesaver, believe me!

Naturally, all this is served in bed along with a robe and a smaller tray of your own to join the royal personage. (No one important eats unattended, you know.) The grander the flurry of activity and fussing, the better—and a photo with crown, scepter, and crumpet in hand (and tray still intact) will be priceless later.

A Silver Paper Crown and Scepter

One Red Rose in a Silver or Crystal Vase

*Equal Amounts of Freshly Squeezed Orange Juice with Ginger-Ale
in a Champagne Flute*

Soft Boiled Eggs in Real Egg Cups

Toasted and Buttered Crumpets with Homemade Jam or Marmalade

Chocolate Dipped Strawberries

Amaretto Coffee

CHOCOLATE DIPPED STRAWBERRIES

Serves 4-6

2 pt. (18-24) strawberries
1 lb. semi-sweet or milk chocolate
kitchen thermometer

1. Wash berries but do not remove leaves. Place berries leaf side down on a cutting board and cut 3/4 way through from top to bottom in 1/8-inch slices.
2. Gently spread slices apart in opposite directions to create a fan shape. Place berries on a wax paper-lined sheet pan and chill for 20-30 minutes.
3. Chop or break chocolate into small pieces and heat in a double-boiler. Melt chocolate slowly and stir constantly.
4. Using a thermometer to keep an eye on the temperature, heat chocolate to 130° (keep stirring). Remove from heat and let cool to 90°.
5. Replace water in bottom of double-boiler and heat to 90°. Maintain this temperature and place chocolate over water.
6. Remove berries from fridge (they should be between 65° and 70°).
7. Hold berry near leaves and dip into chocolate. Place back on pan to cool.
8. When chocolate has set (and just before serving), prepare a plate with a beautiful doily and arrange strawberries in a circular fashion. A few pansies at the center make a loving touch.

BIRTHDAY BREAKFAST PARTY FOR KIDS

I have two sons who cherish a tradition that began in their early childhoods: "The Birthday Breakfast Party." Birthday breakfasts were an offshoot of making sure we could have a perfectly private moment of celebrating the annual milestone together. The regular afternoon party was full of schoolmates, friends, and games.

Chris and Michael are only 15 months apart and, as toddlers, the "unbirthday" boy couldn't understand why he didn't receive presents of his own. So fully wrapped, nonsensical gifts were equally shared early on the birthday morning along with party hats, noisemakers, confetti, and cans of silly string sprayed to their happy hearts' content. A decorated cupcake with a single candle topped off the very special breakfast fare. And by the time we got to the food, they'd been enjoying themselves enough to accept the party dishes as something different from breakfast fare.

Of course, the easiest way to enjoy this personal time is to do everything possible the night before. Wrap the presents. Make the parfaits (cover with plastic wrap and place in freezer). Mix the pancake batter (store in a pitcher in the refrigerator). Put the candle on the cupcake, decorate the table, and get all necessary ingredients ready for the morning.

Don't forget to load film in the camera!

Pancakes in Cookie-Cutter Shapes

Crushed Blueberry Syrup

Crisp Bacon Slices

Hot Chocolate with Marshmallows

Frozen Yogurt Parfaits with Strawberries and Walnuts in a Clear Parfait Glass

Party Hats and Noisemakers

One Cupcake with a Burning Candle

A Few Little Wrapped Presents and Birthday Cards for All Children

PANCAKES

Yield 6-8 pancakes

> 1 C all-purpose flour
> 2 t baking powder
> 1/2 t salt
> 2 T sugar
> 1 egg
> 1 C milk
> 3 T butter or margarine, melted

1. Sift flour with baking powder, salt, and sugar into medium mixing bowl.
2. Beat egg. Add milk and butter. Beat until well mixed.
3. Pour liquid mixture into dry ingredients. Beat only until combined. Batter will be lumpy.
4. Heat griddle, frying pan, or electric skillet. (If using a griddle or skillet that's been cured with cooking oil, there is no need to grease the griddle. A regular skillet will require a little margarine or light oil.) Test temperature by dropping a spoonful of cold water onto the surface. Water should roll off in drops.
5. Pour 1/4 C batter onto griddle for each pancake. Cook until bubbles form on surface and edges become dry. Turn and cook two minutes longer.
6. To make pancakes in shapes, place cookie cutter on cooking surface. Pour batter into cutter. Let set until bubbles appear on surface. Remove cutter and continue cooking until edges are dry. Turn and cook for two more minutes.

CRUSHED BLUEBERRY SYRUP

Makes approximately 1 pint

> 1 pt corn syrup
> 1/2 C fresh blueberries

1. Heat syrup until just hot—about 110°.
2. Puree berries in a processor or blender until just smooth.
3. Mix berries and syrup and remove from heat. Let stand until cool (about 45 minutes).
4. Place mixture in a sealed container and refrigerate overnight.
5. Strain mixture through a sieve or wire strainer.

I prefer to serve syrup hot on fresh pancakes— sprinkling them with a few whole berries I've reserved.

FROZEN YOGURT PARFAITS WITH STRAWBERRIES AND WALNUTS

Serves 6

> 1 pt fresh strawberries
> (reserve 3 to cut in half)
> 1/4 C sugar
> 1 qt frozen vanilla yogurt
> 1 pt whipping cream or Cool Whip
> 3/4 C chopped walnuts
> 3 halved berries for garnish

1. Wash and dice berries.

2. Blend berries and sugar and reserve.
3. In a parfait glass: Spoon a 1" layer of frozen yogurt, then add 1/2" layer of diced strawberries, followed by a second 1" layer of yogurt, then top with a 1/2" layer of chopped walnuts. If space in glass permits, repeat layering until a rounded mound appears at top of glass.
4. Whip cream until thick and spoon on top of dessert. Serve with a strawberry half on very top of cream and sprinkle with finely chopped nuts.

FOR THOSE WHO LOVE OMELETTES

Frittatas in Italy are a "free for all" morning event—a combination of eggs with chopped fresh scallions along with some leftover vegetables or meat from supper last night. In other words, clear out the refrigerator! The fun is that you throw it all together and pop it in a hot oven for just the amount of time you need to toast your favorite bread in the broiler. You'll make a well-timed finish with everything piping hot at once.

> *Broiled Grapefruit*
>
> *Frittata*
>
> *Pumpernickel Toast*
>
> *Cantaloupe with Blueberries and Yogurt*
>
> *Hazelnut Coffee*

BROILED GRAPEFRUIT

> 1/2 grapefruit per person to be served
> 1 T brown sugar per 1/2 grapefruit
> 1 maraschino cherry with stem per 1/2 grapefruit

Place grapefruit on cookie sheet or broiling pan. Sprinkle brown sugar on top of grapefruit. Broil under open flame until sugar is bubbling. Remove from heat. Place cherry in center of grapefruit. Serve hot.

FRITTATA

(Spinach or Zucchini Omelette)
It's a nice "homey" look to use an iron skillet that can go directly from the stove to the oven with just a dash of parmesan and parsley on top. A pretty oven-proof casserole dish can be used too.

Serves 4

> 3 T butter

2 T oil
1 large onion, sliced
2 cloves garlic, sliced lengthwise
2 C cooked spinach or thinly sliced
     par-boiled zucchini
1/4 C parsley, chopped
1/2 t thyme
1/2 t oregano
1 t rosemary
8 eggs
1/2 C grated parmesan cheese
salt and pepper to taste

1. Preheat oven to 350°.

2. In a heavy skillet (that can later be placed in the oven), melt the butter with the oil over moderate heat. Add sliced onion and sliced garlic, and cook until soft but not dark brown. Add spinach or zucchini and all the seasonings. Stir and cook about 10 minutes.

3. In another bowl, beat eggs with a fork until they are just blended. Stir them gently into the spinach/zucchini mixture. Add parmesan cheese.

4. Place frittata in oven and bake until set—about 10 minutes. Serve sliced into wedges.

THE BREAKFAST MEETING

    This sumptuous breakfast is easily manageable by preparing and assembling the tomatoes, juice mixture, fruit slices, and coconut on plates ahead of time. Have the cake baked and the ingredients for the eggs at your fingertips. Premeasure your coffee, and in minutes everything can be on the table! You'll look capable of handling any business just as magically.

Eggs Florentine

Italian Toast Topped with Parmesan and Browned in Broiler

Broiled Tomatoes with Minced Parsley and Parmesan Cheese

Apple Coffee Cake

Banana and Orange Slices Topped with Yogurt and Shredded Coconut

Orange Pineapple Juice

French Vanilla Coffee

EGGS FLORENTINE

Serves 4

For Cream Sauce
    2 T butter
    2 T flour
    1 T cream
    1 C milk
    1 egg yolk
    1/3 C grated Gruyere cheese
    1 package cream spinach (thawed)

For Poached Eggs
    4 eggs
    2 T vinegar

Remember to watch garlic carefully. Garlic should only be cooked until soft and golden brown. If necessary, it should be removed from heat and reserved to be chopped and sprinkled into the dish later in the cooking. If it turns dark brown, it will become bitter.

1. Melt butter in a saucepan and add flour. Slowly whisk in milk and cook, stirring constantly until thickened (about 10 minutes).
2. Whisk cream and egg yolk with 1 T of hot milk mixture to avoid curdling, and then blend into milk.
3. Stir cheese into milk mixture until melted and smooth. Remove from heat.
4. Boil 2 inches of water in a large skillet. Reduce heat until water is calm and add vinegar.
5. Break each egg into separate small cups, and use cups to gently place eggs into water. Poach eggs for 3 to 5 minutes and drain on a paper towel.
6. Heat spinach and use it to line the bottom of a buttered baking dish. Top with eggs and pour sauce over each egg.
7. Broil 3 to 5 minutes and serve.

Just let sauce begin to brown and bubble— and serve immediately.

BROILED TOMATOES WITH MINCED PARSLEY AND PARMESAN CHEESE

Serves 4

>   4 medium tomatoes, halved (or
>   large tomatoes cut in thirds)
>   Lawry's Garlic Salt
>   1/2 C parmesan cheese, grated
>   1/4 C minced parsley
>   pepper to taste
>   sprinkle of oregano

1. Wash and halve tomatoes, and place on aluminum-covered cookie tin or broiler pan.
2. Sprinkle with garlic salt, parmesan cheese (but save some for garnish), parsley, pepper, and oregano.
3. Place in 400° oven for 7 to 10 minutes, until cooked but still firm.
4. Sprinkle again with cheese and pop under the broiler for 1 minute to crisp and melt cheese. Serve immediately.

APPLE COFFEE CAKE

Serves 4

>   1/2 C hot (110°) water
>   1 package active dry yeast
>   2 1/4 C flour
>   1/2 C butter
>   1/4 C sugar
>   1 t salt
>   2 eggs
>   1/2 C brown sugar
>   1/2 C raisins or currents
>   1 1/2 C chopped apple
>   (peeled and cored)
>   1 t cinnamon
>   sprinkle of allspice, nutmeg,
>   cloves to taste
>   9" tube pan

1. Blend water and yeast. Let stand 5 minutes. Stir in 1/2 C flour and let rise 30 minutes at 85°.
2. Beat 1/4 C butter until soft, and blend in sugar and salt. Beat eggs in one at a time.
3. Mix brown sugar, raisins or currents, apple, cinnamon, and remaining butter,

and boil 3 to 5 minutes. Let cool.

4. Blend yeast and butter mixtures and slowly add rest of flour. Beat for 5 minutes and blend in brown sugar and apple mixture. Let rise 2 hours.

5. Push dough down and place in a greased tube pan. Let rise another 30 minutes. Brush top with butter and sprinkle with cinnamon, allspice, nutmeg, and cloves.

6. Bake at 350° for about 30 minutes.

I know many of you feel that getting up early to spend breakfast with friends and family is deprivation of your precious sleep time. But cultivating another opportunity to develop relationships, to communicate, bridge differences, and find common ground, is more than worth the effort. Trust me!

Howard Keel and me as "Clio" in the Broadway musical Saratoga— my first show after West Side Story

A New Year's Eve feast with guests, cast, and crew of the
"Carol Lawrence Show" on Trinity Broadcasting Network

Chapter 3

"The Ladies Who Lunch!"
The Midday Feast

LUNCH IS A MEAL YOU EAT ANYWHERE YOU CAN, WHETHER AT home, at work, or really on the go. It is the midday fuel stop that gets you through the rest of the day.

In planning for midday meals, I have some suggestions that can make preparation easier. As a working mother of two ferociously hungry boys, I always tried to cook in large caldron-sized pots. That way I could freeze four-fifths of whatever I was making in plastic containers and reconstitute it in minutes on my hectic days. Most sauces and soups improve with the freezing and aging process—so I've devised a method of planning ahead and segmenting the various elements of recipes. Here's an example of cookin' big!

Here's to the ladies who lunch. Aren't they unique?

—COMPANY

CHICKEN SOUP (ETCETERA, ETCETERA, ETCETERA)

3 chickens, disjointed, plus liver, hearts, and gizzards
8 fresh scallions, sliced
10 celery sticks, sliced, including leaves
16 carrots, sliced
4 onions, quartered and sliced thinly lengthwise
2 bunches parsley, halved and chopped coarsely
salt and pepper to taste
small fresh bunch of basil or heavy sprinkle dried basil
6 cloves garlic, crushed at the last minute
6 T chicken bullion concentrate

1. In a large, industrial stock pot boil the 3 disjointed chickens, skimming off residue.
2. After 30 minutes, add the ingredients in the order listed and simmer everything 20 minutes until carrots are just cooked but very firm.

You already have an abundance of

The celery leaves always add a delicate flavor.

chicken stock (to de-fat or not, that is your question!) from which you can begin Stracciatelli or Barley soup. Merely reserve the chicken stock and freeze in convenient cubes for later needs. You may want to add the boned meat from the backs and wings for soup garnish and enhancement, but the breasts and legs can provide the major element in a curry, chicken salad, topping to a Caesar salad, stuffing of a crepe, a sandwich, or a cold entree on a hot summer night. The choices for chicken recipes are endless.

3. Serve soup with hot bread and a light salad. Freeze the balance in meal-size plastic resealable bags. These are easy to handle and defrost quickly for unexpected guests or an easy snack.

CREATING THE ULTIMATE LUNCH

The following menus have already been tried "out of town" and back home, to rave reviews.

THE BROWN BAG MENU
(alone or to share)

> *Pasta with Pesto*
> *Poached Chicken Breasts*
> *Carrot, Fennel, Jicama, and Celery Sticks*
> *Italian Sesame Bread Sticks*
> *Whole Sweet Apples*

PASTA WITH PESTO
Serves 4

> 1 lb linguini noodles
> 6 cloves garlic
> 2 large bunches fresh basil leaves
>   (3 C packed)
> 1 C grated parmesan cheese
> 3/4 C olive oil
> 1 t salt
> 1/2 t black pepper

> 1 C chopped walnuts
> 1 C water from cooked linguini
>   (water reserved in pot)
> 1 T olive oil
> 1/4 C walnuts in large chunks
>   to garnish platter

1. Wash, pat dry, and remove stems from basil
2. Measure 3 cups of packed basil and place in blender.
3. Add oil to blender and whip until mixed well.
4. Boil linguini in salted water to which 1 T olive oil is added.
5. Drain linguini and reserve 1-2 C water.
6. Add garlic, cheese, salt, pepper, and walnuts to blender with enough water reserved from boiled linguini to make a thick paste.
7. Return linguini to same pot (still hot!) and begin stirring in pesto sauce, tossing

with 2 large forks. Add a little more hot pasta water to aid coating all linguini with sauce. When all is mixed, pour linguini on platter and sprinkle with parmesan cheese and 1/4 C large chunks of walnuts for decoration. Serve.

POACHED CHICKEN BREASTS

Serves 4

> 4 boneless, skinless chicken breasts
> 1 C white wine
> 2 C chicken stock or water
> 4 cloves garlic
> 2 bay leaves
> 1 t peppercorns

1. Spread breasts on a cutting board and pound lightly to flatten.
2. Smash garlic flat with the blade of a chef's knife.
3. Place wine, stock, garlic, bay leaves, and peppercorns in a covered skillet and heat.
4. When liquid begins to steam add chicken. Poach 12 to 15 minutes until cooked through. (Be careful not to let the liquid boil.)
5. Remove chicken from liquid and drain. Place in a resealable bag and chill in the refrigerator until cold. The chicken breasts are ready for your brown bag lunch.

ITALIAN SESAME BREAD STICKS

Makes 12 sticks

Make a double batch of Italian Sesame Bread Sticks and store in tall, airtight glass jars. They make a great decoration for your kitchen or add a big red bow and give to your favorite person for no reason at all.

For Dough:

> 1 cake yeast, softened in 1/4 C
> lukewarm water (let yeast
> stand 5 to 10 minutes)
> 2 C warm water
> 1 t salt
> 5-6 C flour

For Coating:

> 1 egg
> 1 T milk
> sesame seeds

1. In large bowl combine water, salt, and 3 C flour. Mix well.
2. Add softened yeast and beat mixture until very smooth.
3. Mix in remaining flour to make soft dough. Turn mixture onto lightly floured board. Knead until dough is smooth and elastic.
4. Shape dough into smooth ball, and place in large, greased bowl, turning to lightly coat the dough.
5. Cover bowl with waxed paper and towel. Let stand in a warm place until dough is doubled in size (about 2 hours).
6. Punch dough down with fist. Knead again on lightly floured board for about 3 minutes.
7. Lightly roll dough into two rectangles 1/4" thick and about 6" wide. Cut into 1" wide strips, and use palm of hand to roll strips

to pencil thickness, stretching dough to about 8" lengths.

8. Brush strips lightly with a mixture of 1 egg slightly beaten with 1 T milk, then roll in bowl of sesame seeds. Place strips 1" apart on greased baking sheets and twist.

Cover lightly with towel and let rise in warm place until double in size.

9. Bake at 425° for 5 minutes. Reduce heat to 350° and bake 15 minutes or until sticks are browned and crisp all the way through. Do not overbake.

A LITTLE ITALIAN LUNCH

Like the whole world, I've laughed at and loved Bob Hope since I was a kid. He and Bing Crosby took us *all* along whatever road they traveled with Dorothy Lamour in those great movie comedies! Hope's slick black hair and knowing wisecracks belie his warm and generous heart. He is every GI Joe's favorite buddy due to hundreds of USO shows in war zones all over the world. I've had the honor of doing many live and televised shows with Bob, and his ad-libs during rehearsals are a hundred times funnier than the expensive lines he has written for him.

On one occasion when I was working with Bob, I wanted to do a scene and number from the production of *Funny Girl*. It was Fanny Brice's bold audition for Florenz Ziegfeld. (When I was working on the road in *Funny Girl*, I had fallen in love with the young Fanny Brice.) The only problem was that I needed a "Ziegfeld" to help me set up Fanny's brash tenacity. Now, who could lend more validity and importance to playing Ziegfeld than Mr. Hope himself? But how do you ask Bob Hope to play straight to you?!

Well, I asked, and without a second's hesitation he agreed.

On the day of taping, I brought a large pan of one of his favorite dishes—Eggplant Parmigiano—and my sons and I shared lunch with the great impresario Florenz Ziegfeld as portrayed by the biggest and most generous star in my book, Mr. Bob Hope!

Here's how you can make Hope's favorite dish (and the accompanying dishes) for your favorite stars!

Bob Hope and me in a TV special— "The Road to Somewhere"!

Eggplant Parmigiano

Caesar Salad

Italian Bread with Michael's Roasted Garlic Spread

EGGPLANT PARMIGIANO
Serves 4

Since time for lunch is usually short, it's best to make this ahead of time and freeze 4 servings in one container. (Freezing actually improves the flavor.)

> 1 lb eggplant
> 3 eggs, beaten
> 1 C all-purpose flour
> 3/4 C light oil
> 4 C spaghetti sauce
> 2 mozzarella cheeses,
>   sliced and shredded
> 1 C parmesan cheese, grated
> 1/4 C Italian parsley, chopped

1. Wash and slice eggplant thinly, crosswise.
2. Dip slices in egg and then dredge in flour.
3. Sauté slices in oil until golden brown. (If oil becomes dark, discard and start with fresh oil.)
4. Drain eggplant on paper towels to absorb excess oil.
5. Ladle enough sauce to cover the bottom of a 9"x 9"x 2" baking dish.
6. Place one layer of eggplant on top of sauce.
7. Sprinkle with parmesan cheese.
8. Cover with layer of mozzarella.
9. Add another layer of sauce.
10. Repeat steps 6 to 9, ending with sauce and two cheeses. Sprinkle with chopped Italian parsley.
11. Cover with aluminum foil, place on a cookie sheet (to catch drips from the sauce) and bake at 350° for 1 hour.
12. Remove from oven and allow to sit for 5

minutes. Do let this cool and set up before cutting so you can have sturdy squares—not shapeless piles!

CAESAR SALAD
Serves 4

> 1 large head Romaine lettuce
> 1 coddled egg
> 1/2 C olive oil
> 3-4 large cloves of garlic
> 2-3 anchovy fillets
> 3 T Dijon mustard
> 3 T lemon juice
> 2 dashes Worcestershire sauce
> sprinkle of freshly ground pepper
> 3/4 C parmesan cheese

Croutons

> 1/2 C margarine
> 2 cloves sliced garlic
> 4 slices Italian bread cut in
>   1" cubes
> parmesan cheese

1. Separate leaves of Romaine, wash, pat dry, and layer on large paper towels. Wrap in a moist dish cloth or seal in resealable bags and refrigerate until ready to serve.
2. Boil egg for 1 1/2 minutes and set aside.
3. In a cold wooden bowl, crush anchovies and garlic in oil until smooth.
4. Add and mix egg, Dijon mustard, lemon juice, Worcestershire sauce, pepper, and parmesan cheese.

Croutons (may be made ahead of time)
5. Melt margarine and heat garlic; do not burn.
6. Cube bread and toss in margarine and

It is wise to slice the eggplant, salt both sides and place in a large bowl with a heavy plate to weigh it down. Let stand for 2 hours. That will remove much of the water in the eggplant and allow it to cook without being soggy.

A coddled egg is an egg placed whole in boiling water for 1½ minutes. This partially cooks the egg and kills any bacteria.

garlic until golden brown. Sprinkle and toss with parmesan in the pan. Remove and reserve.

Assembling the Caesar Salad

7. Remove Romaine from towels, tear into large bite-size pieces with your hands, and place in wooden bowl. Toss well so that all leaves are coated with the dressing. Add croutons and an extra sprinkling of parmesan cheese. Serve on chilled plates.

MICHAEL'S ROASTED GARLIC SPREAD
Yields approximately 1/2 C garlic paste

>   1 large head of garlic
>   1 C olive oil

1. Separate cloves of garlic, but do not peel the individual cloves.
2. Place cloves in a shallow glass baking dish and barely cover with olive oil.
3. Bake at 275° for about 1 1/4 hours. Cloves should be browned, not burned. Remove from oven and set aside to cool.
4. Remove cloves with a slotted spoon and drain on a paper towel.
5. Holding cloves between thumb and fore-finger, squeeze out garlic.
6. Mash softened cloves with a little olive oil to form paste.
7. Store in a sealed container.

THE BUSINESS MEETING LUNCH
I cooked this meal for the publisher of this book—and he loved it!

> ### Linguini with Clam Sauce
> ### Spinach Salad
> ### Hard Rolls
> ### Whole Fruit Sorbet with Raspberries
> ### Amaretto Cookies

LINGUINI WITH CLAM SAUCE
Serves 4

>   4 or 5 cans (5 1/2 oz) chopped clams
>   8 cloves garlic
>   1 bunch Italian parsley, chopped
>   1 stick low-fat margarine
>   1/2 C safflower oil
>   salt
>   pepper
>   3/4 C chopped walnuts (reserve 1/4 C in larger chunks for garnish)
>   1 lb linguini
>   1 C parmesan cheese

1. Open cans of clams, drain and reserve clam juice in a separate container.
2. Peel garlic and slice thinly, lengthwise.
3. Wash parsley, discard stems, and chop coarsely.
4. Place margarine and oil in large skillet and add garlic. Sauté on medium heat until golden. Remove garlic and reserve.
5. Add clams and parsley to pan and simmer 5 minutes. Salt and pepper to taste.
6. Add clam juice and garlic and simmer slowly for 10 minutes. Set aside.
7. Boil linguini in salted water with 2 T oil until firm (but not well done).
8. Strain and roll on a platter sprinkled with parmesan cheese.
9. Add 1/2 C of nuts to clam sauce and mix well. Reserve remaining nuts to garnish top of linguini.

10. Pour 3/4 of sauce on linguini and toss well. Place on platter.
11. Arrange remainder of sauce on top of linguini, with parmesan, nuts, and a garnish of parsley.
12. Serve hot.

SPINACH SALAD

Serves 4

    2 bunches fresh spinach

    1 medium can water chestnuts, sliced

    3 hard-boiled eggs, diced coarsely

    4 slices crisp bacon, diced

           (or you can use Bacon Bits)

Dressing

    1/2 C sugar

    1/2 C catsup

    1/4 C vinegar

    1 t salt

    1/2 C oil

    1 t Worcestershire sauce

    1 medium white onion, sliced

1. Tear spinach into pieces after washing and blotting dry.
2. Add water chestnuts and eggs.
3. Fry bacon crisp, drain on paper towels, then crumble and set aside.
4. Make dressing by combining dressing ingredients in a jar with a lid. Shake well.
5. Before serving salad, add bacon and then toss with dressing.
6. Serve on chilled plates or in a large salad bowl.

THE PORTABLE LUNCH

Although a Broadway show looks like a small slice of life in a two-hour compressed capsule, the number of people required to bring it to a polished performance is staggering. Some stagehands never even cross your path during the show because they work in the catwalk above your head or in the spotlight booth. In addition, the musicians, wardrobe people, business managers, press people, hairdressers, makeup artists, doormen, and more all make this major illusion a reality every night.

I was in *Kiss of the Spider Woman* on Broadway. Because the subject matter was very heavy and the really demanding singing and dancing role was exhileratingly exhausting and dangerous, I felt closer to my dance partners than usual. Also, the entire company made me feel so warmly welcomed when I replaced Chita Rivera that I wanted to do something really *special* for each person at Christmastime.

I couldn't afford to shop that extensively for appropriate gifts for everyone, so I decided to personally bake so sumptuous a morsel that it would be an unforgettable and unsurpassed taste treat—decadently delicious.

My dear sister-in-law Mary Lou gave me her recipe for "Seven-Layer Crunch," and it more than satisfied my search for the perfect Christmas gift. It defies sensible calorie counting and healthy guidelines, but it sets a new record for richness. It layers and bakes on a cookie sheet a stick of margarine, graham crackers, chocolate chips, vanilla chips, butterscotch chips, pecans, shredded coconut, and condensed milk. One piece leaves a person puzzled at who would dare to combine so many favorite flavors and crunchies into one entity!

I began baking sheets of this delicacy one night and, after cutting them into squares, I wrapped each piece in bright holiday paper, tied a proper ribbon around it, and attached a "To" and "From" card for every person I knew connected to the Broadhurst Theatre. As I handed them out, I hugged my fellow cast and crew members, wishing them a glorious Christmas. The ones who couldn't wait tasted the treats and almost flipped. They couldn't believe they were homemade!

I guess my biggest kick came from the dancing boys' dressing room. That night they did the most frenzied, never-ceasing, high-energy Latin number I've ever seen! They attributed the surge of strength and energy to that square of sweets and the loving effort that wished them a merry Christmas from my kitchen and my heart!

Another wonderful memory is associated with the time I played the lead in *Kiss of the Spider Woman*. This is a lunch I loved having between matinee and evening shows at the Broadhurst Theatre during production.

> *You don't need to boil the shrimp. Merely letting them stand in the hot water is enough to cook them perfectly. Never, never overcook shrimp. It only toughens them.*

---

*Shrimp with Remoulade Sauce
Bean and Mushroom Salad
Cheese-Stuffed Rice Balls
Hot Italian Bread
Seven-Layer Crunch*

SHRIMP WITH REMOULADE SAUCE
Serves 6

2 lb fresh, medium-sized raw shrimp
1/4 C chopped onion
2 cloves garlic, smashed flat
1 bay leaf
1 C mayonnaise
1 T minced pickle or relish
2 t Dijon mustard
1 T minced parsley
1/2 t tarragon
1/2 t chervil
1/2 t anchovy paste

1. Simmer onion, garlic, and bay leaf in 2 quarts water for 5 minutes.
2. Add shrimp and turn off heat and cover for an additional 5 minutes. Remove shrimp and chill.
3. Make sauce by blending mayonnaise, pickle, Dijon mustard, parsley, tarragon, chervil, and anchovy paste together. Chill.
4. Shell and de-vein shrimp, leaving just the end of the tail on. Serve with chilled sauce.

BEAN AND MUSHROOM SALAD
Serves 4 to 6

1 lb fresh mushrooms

1 C navy or northern beans
1 C kidney beans
1/3 C chopped parsley
French Vinaigrette Dressing (p. 40)

1. Remove stems and peel skins from mushrooms. Cut in 1/2" slices.
2. Rinse beans and drain well.
3. Toss all with dressing, saving a few sprigs of parsley for garnish.

CHEESE-STUFFED RICE BALLS

Serves 4 to 6

It's fun to break Cheese-Stuffed Rice Balls apart and watch the surprise of those not expecting the cheese center!

2 eggs
2 C cold, cooked rice
4 oz mozzarella cheese
      (cut in 1/2" cubes)
3/4 C fine, dry bread crumbs
1/4 C grated parmesan cheese
vegetable oil for deep frying

1. Beat 2 eggs lightly with fork.
2. Add 2 C cold rice (leftovers are great). Stir gently; don't mash rice.
3. Scoop 1 T rice in spoon.
4. Place 1 cube mozzarella cheese in middle.
5. Top with another spoonful and press together.
6. Drop into dish of plain bread crumbs.
7. Cover ball with bread crumbs and place on wax paper on a cookie sheet.
8. Refrigerate for at least 30 minutes (preferably longer).
9. Heat oil in deep fat fryer to 375°.

10. Preheat oven to 250°.
11. Line baking dish with paper towels to drain cheeseballs.
12. Fry rice balls (4 to 5 at once) for 5 minutes, or until golden brown, and drain.
13. Transfer rice balls to baking dish and keep warm in oven.
14. Serve as soon as possible. Although these are spectacular hot, they hold their shape and taste terrific cold as well!

SEVEN-LAYER CRUNCH

graham crackers
a stick of margarine
12-oz bag of chocolate chips
12-oz bag of vanilla chips
12-oz bag of butterscotch chips
12 oz chopped pecans
12-oz bag of shredded coconut
1 medium can condensed milk

1. Melt margarine and spread evenly on bottom of cookie sheet. Cover bottom of sheet with layer of whole graham crackers (this becomes the crust).
2. Layer on cookie sheet of graham crackers each 12-oz package of chocolate chips, vanilla chips, butterscotch chips, pecans, and coconut (in that order and evenly distributed). Pour condensed milk over all.
3. Bake at 350° for 10 to 12 minutes or until all ingredients are melted.
4. Cool for approximately 5 minutes so it firms up to cut easily into thick-chewy-but-top-crusty squares.
    Caution: If bars cool too long, you won't be able to cut them.

Be careful to test and cut the "Seven-Layer Crunch" before it hardens and becomes unmanageable (rather like cutting toffee).

I
Remember
Pasta

THERE'S ALWAYS PIZZA LUNCH!

One of the most essential parts of hosting a telethon is putting your guests at ease at once. When speaking to a child—especially a disabled child—a real tenderness is demanded. I've always loved working ahead of time with any of the kids I'd be interviewing in a telethon. That way the crazy circuslike arena of a television studio doesn't overwhelm and frighten the children.

I usually have the children over to my home for a lunch of their choice of Italian food—from spaghetti to pizza. I did that for Susie Evie, the poster-child of the Cerebral Palsy Telethon I was hosting in Los Angeles one year. Susie, a blonde five-year-old angel who resembled a Shirley Temple collectible doll, was imprisoned in heavy steel braces to her hips. Because she had fallen painfully so many times when attempting to walk, she refused to ever try again.

As Susie and I struggled to eat the hot pizza without ruining our clothes, we became good friends. She adored brownies, like all kids do. During the afternoon we rehearsed how I would kneel beside her and hold her up while we spoke or I sang to her. With pizza, brownies, popsicles, and laughter she was more than at ease and I was grateful for the time we shared!

Sure enough, Susie turned into a real pro as the long night wore on. During the show she saw me tap dancing up and down a set of stairs in a tribute to the "King of Taps," Bill Robinson. She had never seen such a combination of rhythm, music, and antics on stairs, and her eyes were wide as saucers. As I ran off stage to change my costume, she reached for me and I picked her up. "I want to do that," she gasped.

"O.K. Susie," I said and looked her straight in the eye, "when you are out of your braces and walking, I'll teach you to tap dance. I promise."

Before I could catch my breath, the telethon was in its last minutes. Susie and I were doing the closing as planned—I knelt beside her and sang, "You and Me Against the World"—when Susie suddenly whispered, "I want to walk."

Well, it was my turn to be wide-eyed. I stopped the orchestra and said to the audience, "Susie just said she wants to walk, and I know we'd all like to see her." A hush fell over the house, and I steadied her on her feet and then moved back a bit.

I tried to stay calm, knowing we only had seconds left on the clock. "Here are my hands, Susie, come on." Her blue eyes never left mine, and she straightened her little back. Then she reached forward and swung her right foot up. It hit the floor loudly as she pushed the left one, too. She started to fall, but she grabbed my hands as I caught her in my arms.

It was then I heard her really laugh for the first time. The studio erupted into pandemonium and we rolled the credits. I know someone on high was writing the script that night, and I'll never forget it.

Pizza Lawrence Style

Serves 4 to 6

    1 package hot roll mix
    1 medium can tomato sauce
    sprinkle oregano
    3/4 C parmesan cheese
    1/8 t black pepper
    sprinkle dried or 1/4 C fresh chopped
        basil
    1/3 C oil
    6 cloves garlic, minced
    1 C shredded mozzarella cheese

1. Follow directions on hot roll mix container.
2. Allow to rise one hour.
3. Flatten and roll into circle (16" diameter).
4. Spread ingredients over rolled out dough, beginning with the tomato sauce. Add each item in order, ending with the oil dribble on top. Evenly distribute the minced garlic over the pizza.
5. Bake in preheated oven at 425° for 40 minutes. Remove. Let cool for a minute and serve.

Joey's Chopped Salad

Serves 6 to 8

    1/2 head romaine lettuce
    1/2 head iceberg lettuce
    two oranges, peeled and sectioned
    1 red onion, sliced in rounds
    3/4 C raisins
    1/2 C chopped walnuts

1. Wash lettuces and break into bite-size pieces.
2. Place in large salad bowl.
3. Add oranges.
4. Peel and slice onion in half lengthwise and then in rounds; add to bowl.
5. Toss in raisins and nuts and mix well with "Mike's Salad Dressing."

Mike's Salad Dressing

Serves 6 to 8

    3/4 C light oil
    1/4 C olive oil
    2 T Dijon mustard
    4 cloves garlic crushed
    1 egg
    1/4 C lemon juice
    salt and pepper to taste

Mix ingredients together with wire whisk and toss in salad.

No-Fat Brownies

Makes 12 to 16 brownies

    2/3 C unbleached flour
    1/3 C cocoa
    1 1/2 unsweetened baking
        chocolate squares
    1 T canola oil
    6 extra large egg whites
    1 1/4 C sugar
    3/4 C unsweetened applesauce
    1/2 C nonfat yogurt
    1 t vanilla

1. Sift together flour and cocoa. Set aside.
2. Melt chocolate in a double boiler. When melted, add oil and mix until combined. Set aside to cool slightly.
3. Beat egg whites with sugar until very fluffy. Add applesauce, yogurt, vanilla, melted chocolate, and dry ingredients.
4. Beat until well combined.
5. Spray 9"x 9" baking pan with oil (or use a non-stick pan). Pour mixture into pan.
6. Bake at 350° for 20 to 25 minutes. Mixture will feel firm, but toothpick inserted will come out covered with batter, not clean. These are *moist*.
7. Remove from oven. Chill. Cut in squares and serve.

It's best to cut pizza with a rolling wheel cutter—but if you don't have one on hand, a pair of kitchen shears will keep the cheese from losing its place on the pizza.

These brownies are delicious, low-fat, and cholesterol-free besides. Great for all kids!

PLAYBILL
a weekly magazine for theatregoers

Winter Garden

SARATOGA

St. James Theatre

PLAYBILL
a weekly magazine for theatregoers

SUBWAYS ARE FOR SLEEPING

Brooks Atkinson Theatre

PLAYBILL
a weekly magazine for theatregoers

NIGHT LIFE

Three of the plays I was in after
<u>West Side Story</u>—each a wonderful
memory and delight!

Chapter 4

That's Entertainment

Memories of Dinner at My House

A DINNER PARTY IS THE GREATEST OF SHOWS. IN MY CHILDHOOD, people fasted for days before coming to our home for one of my mother's "simple" dinners—which ran between seven and nine courses and took three hours to savor … and survive!

On one such evening, a particularly robust lady (let's just call her Theresa Marrisi) came ready to critique every bite. She was quite overweight and, unfortunately for her, equally vain. So she corsetted herself up enough to shame even Diamond Lil and began eating the first course of stuffed mushrooms and bacon-ringed chicken livers. Then came baked clams, pepperoni, salami, pimento, stuffed celery and olives, followed by piping hot Stracciatelli soup full of shredded chicken. A crisp salad of every imaginable crunchy vegetable was accompanied by the thinnest homemade cheese garlic bread in large pieces. (It was so fragile you had to hold it carefully.) She consumed many!

The ravioli my mother made were always oversized and filled with an undefinable but delicious combination of meats and cheeses of many varieties. Just when you thought you recognized them all, the tenderness of the dough knocked you out and foiled your computations; so you'd just have to bite into the next ravioli, and try again.

Now, spaghetti sauce is authentically and lovingly referred to as "gravy" by Italians in our town. Some of the most delectable, mouth-melting tastes were ceremoniously (if not religiously) married for an entire day of simmering bliss in Mom's giant pot, affectionately nudged and turned all the while—until *she* proclaimed, "Finished!" A huge platter was necessary to accommodate the variety of meats that lent their essences to the gravy. There were always meatballs (ground beef, pork, and veal), lamb, pork ribs,

The clown with his pants falling down, Or the dance that's a dream of romance, or the scene where the villain is mean … that's entertainment!

—BAND WAGON

neck bones, beef roast with bones, sausage, chicken, and sometimes squab.

Then, as if no one had touched a bit of food, a turkey dinner appeared, complete with mashed potatoes, hot rolls, candied yams, incredible dressing, creamed brussels sprouts, and cranberry sauce. Mama would then take away the dirty dishes and serve a three-layered Jello fantasy: fresh fruit with a custard cheese layer plus a refreshing sliced orange salad and dew-dropped wedges of fresh anise.

At about this time, our guest, Theresa, thought we were close to dessert, so she asked for more Jello. She didn't realize Mama was merely cleaning everyone's palate and getting her second wind. I was told to put out new plates and help serve the stuffed Eggplant Parmesan with the greatest Chicken Cacciatore anyone ever ate anywhere!

We didn't know that Chicken Cacciatore was Theresa's weakness. Her eyes grew as wide as the plates being passed to her. She loaded up and started eating at a faster clip than anyone else—but not for long! She suddenly gazed across the table with the strangest look on her face. Her eyes glazed over, closed, and *plop*! Her head fell forward into her dish, and she was up to her ears in Chicken Cacciatore! There was a stunned silence, and then everyone jumped up and struggled to lift her head out of the food and her limp body out of the chair. They escorted her to the powder room, where three ladies unlaced her girdle and threw one of my father's robes on her. Then two husky men carried her outside to the winter-fresh air to revive her and walk her back to life.

I was a frightened nine-year-old. I ran to my mom in the kitchen, "Mom, I was so scared that Theresa would die!" "Oh, she'd never die," Mama grinned, "but she sure liked my Chicken Cacciatore." My mom was thrilled to tears, of course. What a compliment to her culinary skills—and a great story besides! Now *that's* entertainment!

Me as a Prima Ballerina in the Christmas TV special "The Enchanted Nutcracker"

OPENING NIGHT
THE ULTIMATE
SPAGHETTI DINNER

You certainly don't need to feel that your dinners must be as extravagant as my mother's! Remember, everyone's signature style is different. You *can*, however, put together your own ultimate dinner experience with a little work and some help from the recipes and tips in this chapter. I've included everything from the appetizers down to the secret of my own "gravy" recipe—and ideas to make the entire evening an event your guests won't soon forget. This is the actual show, or new production, *you* make happen. It is the opening night of your loving effort—just as company dinners were to my mom. It encapsulates my philosophy about cooking for anyone, and satisfies my joy and need to please my audience—*you*!!! I've included the script for the dinner. The jargon will be theatrical, but that's what makes it fun! Let's get started!!!

CREATING THE SHOW

Everyone who comes for a meal arrives hungry. When my mother used to talk of having a restaurant, she wanted to have dishes of hot appetizers at the door for people. Appetizers are a way of saying "I love you" right from the start. And there are many simple finger foods that allow the hungry guest to relax and begin to enjoy the evening immediately.

I usually have an assortment of appetizers available on the kitchen table and counter so that when I enlist my guests to help create the meal, I also begin to take care of them. Here are some of my favorites—and some treasures that carry on my Italian traditions. They are like the playbill, T shirts, and souvenirs in the lobby of Broadway theatres. They whet your imagination for what lies ahead when the curtain goes up!

I
Remember
Pasta

ANTIPASTO SALAD PLATTER WITH FRENCH VINAIGRETTE DRESSING AND ROASTED GARLIC PASTE

Serves 6 to 8

> 1 head red lettuce
> 1/2 C French Vinaigrette Dressing
> (recipe p. 40)
> 1/2 C Roasted Garlic Paste
> (recipe p. 40)
> 1/2 lb mozzarella cheese
> 1/2 lb Cappacola (Italian Ham)
> 1/2 lb dry salami
> 2 sweet red peppers
> 1 bunch scallions
> 1 C red radishes
> 1 pt cherry tomatoes
> 1 C kalmata olives

1. Wash lettuce and separate leaves.
2. On a large platter, arrange the leaves as a base, with the edges hanging slightly over the edge.
3. Place two small bowls on the platter and fill one with the dressing and one with the roasted garlic paste.
4. Cut cheese, peppers, and scallions into 1"x 2" long sticks. Roll slices of cold meats into cigars shapes of same length.
5. Wash and trim radishes; cut into rose design.
6. Wash and dry cherry tomatoes.
7. Arrange all items: cheeses, meats, peppers, scallions, radishes, tomatoes, and olives in a decorative pattern on the platter.
8. Tightly cover with plastic wrap and refrigerate until ready to serve.

FRENCH VINAIGRETTE DRESSING

Yield 1 cup

> 3/4 C olive or walnut oil
> 1/4 C red wine vinegar
> 1/2 t each salt and pepper
> 1 t Dijon mustard

1. Combine all ingredients in medium-size mixing bowl.
2. Whisk all ingredients together thoroughly.
3. Store in a sealed container and refrigerate until serving.

ROASTED GARLIC PASTE

Yield 1/2 cup

> 1 large head of garlic
> 1 C olive oil

1. Separate cloves of garlic but do not peel the individual cloves.
2. Place cloves in a shallow glass baking dish and barely cover with olive oil.
3. Bake at 275° for about 1 1/4 hours. Cloves should be browned but not burned. Remove from oven and set aside to cool.
4. Remove cloves with a slotted spoon (save oil for salad) and drain on paper towel.
5. Holding cloves between thumb and forefinger, squeeze out garlic.
6. Mash softened cloves with a little olive oil to form paste.
7. Store in a sealed container.

BAKED RICOTTA

Serves 6 to 8

>1 lb low-fat ricotta cheese
>coarsely ground black pepper
>plain melba toast (long or
>rounds)

1. Place ricotta in a small, shallow, oven-proof dish. Spread the cheese into a thin, even layer to the edge of the dish.
2. Coat entire layer of ricotta with coarsely ground black pepper. Pepper coating should be thick enough to "hide" the ricotta.
3. Bake at 400° about 1 hour or until ricotta is quite dry.
4. Time it so it comes out when guests arrive. It's best hot but still tasty cold.

HOT SCALLION, CHEESE, AND CRAB DIP

>8 oz Velveeta cheese
>small bunch scallions, chopped in
>rounds
>4 oz crab meat (or a processed
>look-alike fish)
>1 loaf French bread, cut into small
>chunks for dipping

1. Melt cheese in a double boiler until easy to stir.
2. Wash, trim, and cut scallions in rounds 1/4" thick, including as much of greens as possible.
3. Break up crab or imitation crab meat into bite-size pieces.

4. Stir scallions and crab into hot cheese mixture. Mix well and pour into chafing dish with a lit candle under it to keep it hot.
5. Put sliced bread into serving basket and encourage guests to break bread and dip into the cheese, making sure to get some crab and scallion, too.

STUFFED CELERY

Serves 6 to 8

>1 bunch celery
>1 8 oz package of nonfat cream
>cheese
>sprinkle of paprika

1. Wash and trim celery stalks, leaving leaves intact.
2. Spread cream cheese into bottom of each stalk so it is even with the edges.
3. Arrange on a serving dish and sprinkle with paprika.

QUICK PIZZA TOAST

Serves 6 to 8

>1 loaf Italian bread
>8 oz canned tomato, marinara,
>or meat sauce
>1/2 lb shredded mozzarella cheese

1. Cut bread in half lengthwise.
2. Spread on sauce and sprinkle with cheese.
3. Broil until cheese melts and is slightly browned. Cut in 2" slices and serve.

SAUCE—
IT'S A PERSONAL THING

The sauce evolves with each individual's touch and particular taste. Though all of my mother's five sisters were taught by my singin', dancin', adorable Nana, they each turned out totally different gravy. My practical and frugal Aunt Mary had thinner gravy and it was usually meatball sparse when seconds were requested. My ebullient mother's gravy seemed capable of feeding the multitudes, even when they turned up by surprise. My Aunt Ange, who's husband Charlie was an avid fisherman, very often shifted the meat to fish fillets or even canned tuna. You get the idea—everyone's "gravy" is unique.

Having left home early and being thousands of miles away from Mama's hands-on coaching, I, in turn, have changed the original recipe slightly. So it is with tremendous pride (and a silent request for my mother's forgiveness and understanding for revealing all her secrets) that I present my gravy!

I urge you to make as large an amount as your pots can produce because it takes as much time for two cups as for two tons (well, maybe a little more). The gravy becomes the foundation for a million meat and vegetable entrees and side dishes—and it improves with freezing!

STUFFED CLAMS
Serves 4 to 6

    16 fresh clams or 2 cans (6 oz)
        chopped clams; 16 clam
        shells
    1/2 C Italian bread crumbs
    1/4 C Parmesan cheese
2 cloves garlic, crushed
2 T chopped Italian parsley
sprinkle of black pepper

1. Wash and open clams, using 1/2 clam on each shell (loosening clam from shells). If using chopped clams, divide evenly among 16 shells.
2. Mix together bread crumbs, cheese, garlic, parsley, and pepper and sauté in oil for a few minutes.
3. Put approximately 1 t of bread mixture on each shell and bake at 350° for 15 minutes. Serve hot.

CAST, CONTENTS, PROPS, PRODUCER'S NOTES, AND STAGE DIRECTION

As my mom created a stage for her shows, let's establish the parallel and label our show in "theatrical terms." The "Cast" will be the starring dishes of the menu—the "contents" will be the ingredients necessary—the "script" will be the preparation accompanied by "stage directions." Of course, what is a show without special notes of correction and fine-tuning by the "Producer"? Now, before the curtain can go up on the stage, we must prepare or rehearse the script, and here's a great hit anytime … anywhere:

CAROL'S SPAGHETTI SAUCE (THE DIVA)

PRODUCER'S NOTES:

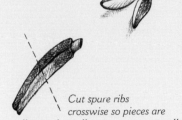

Slice garlic like this:

Cut spure ribs crosswise so pieces are small enough to allow guests to taste all the various meats.

Take note of how boney the meats are—my peasant forefathers never could afford expensive cuts, but took the tougher meats and cooked them longer and more lovingly, stirring in clever spices so everything really came out better in the end (sounds like an Italian fable … sort of!).

Tearing leaves keeps basil from bruising; they sing better then!

I know these are large proportions, but I cook for "armies" and to freeze some meals for the future! You can always reduce this recipe to half the amounts.

My absolutely most cherished cooking utensil is the hand-carved, 20"-long wooden spoon my grandfather gave to my mother on her wedding day. The thoughtful gesture of personally creating the most important tool for a new Italian bride was a ritual begun with the first of his six daughters, which he was forced to repeat for each succeeding one. Each spoon was different and commanded a place of honor and easy access in every kitchen. My mom's spoon stands above all the other favorites I use daily. It is on my stove counter at my fingertips—and in a special place in my heart!

CAST AND CONTENTS:

10 garlic cloves, sliced thickly

3/4 cup light Wesson oil

1 1/2 lb country spare ribs cut in half by butcher

2 lbs lamb shanks cut in thirds by butcher

2 lbs chuck roast with bone, cut in 2" squares by butcher

2-3 veal bones

2-3 pork neck bones

2-3 lamb neck bones

1 large (28 oz) can crushed tomatoes

1 large (28 oz) can tomato puree

1 large (28 oz) can plum tomatoes (chopped well)

2 large (12 oz) cans tomato paste

9 cups of water (proportion of water to tomato paste is 3 to 1)

1 medium bunch fresh basil (leaves only) torn by hand in large pieces

1 large bunch Italian parsley (leaves only, chopped in large pieces)

3 T coarsely ground black pepper

3 T salt

4 T sugar

4 large cloves of garlic, crushed

1/2 cup grated Parmesan cheese

3" x 2" wedge of romano cheese, whole

1/3 cup dried basil

4 bay leaves, broken in half

SCRIPT:

1. Brown all garlic until golden in large skillet and reserve.

2. Wash and pat dry all meats.

3. Sprinkle meats liberally with Lawry's garlic salt and black pepper (coarse).

4. Brown all sides of meat in hot oil and reserve in large stock pot.

5. Mix the three kinds of canned tomatoes in large bowl.

6. Pour as much of the tomato mixture into the large skillet in which you browned the meat. Put in as much as the skillet will allow.

7. Pour remainder of tomato mixture and water into stock pot with cooked meat.

8. Heat and stir (freeing bits of meat from bottom of skillet with wooden spoon).

9. Add parsley, basil, and seasonings to skillet; stir well and bring to a simmer; adjust seasoning to your personal taste. Place a heat diffuser under stockpot.

10. Pour mixture into stock pot until 3/4 full (if you have too much mixture for your stock pot, divide kinds of meats proportionately and cook in additional pots).

11. Bring all to a rolling boil and then lower the heat to just a slow simmer. Cook for at least 2 1/2 hours, or until beef and lamb are tender. Don't forget to add the reserved garlic to the pot!

Note that ingredients match the script, parallel to each direction. This is how an actor maps out his script.

A heat diffuser is most important because tomato sauce becomes bitter if burned. And the heavy pieces of meat will always burn unless stirred often and protected by the diffuser.

I Remember *Pasta*

Just when you thought it was safe to leave the kitchen, we begin step 2!

PRODUCER'S NOTES:	CAST AND CONTENTS:	SCRIPT:
I prefer small meatballs, so a person can sample a variety of meats in the sauce. Sometimes chicken can be added, or squab, or veal—they present subtle differences. Experiment for yourself!	5 cloves of garlic, sliced lengthwise 3/4 C Wesson oil 6 lbs ground meat (3 lbs beef, 3 lbs pork) 1 C Italian parsley 6 eggs 1 1/2 C breadcrumbs	1. Sauté garlic in large skillet with oil until golden brown. Remove and add to simmering gravy. 2. Mix all ingredients in large bowl and form into meatballs, 1 1/2" to 2" in diameter. 3. Brown meatballs in garlic oil already in skillet. Cover while cooking on one side, then continually turn so that all sides are brown and crusty.
A sautéed meatball is the only way I like meatballs. As a child, I was a sick and finicky eater and refused to touch "red" meatballs (ones that had been in the gravy). My Nana (and my mom too) always saved my meatballs separately till dinner was served. They do make quite an entree, folks!	1 3/4 C parmesan cheese, grated a generous sprinkling of black pepper (1/4 C) 15 cloves garlic, minced salt to taste	4. Remove from skillet and place in covered bowl. 5. Continue to simmer gravy, adjusting seasonings and tasting beef for tenderness. When beef is almost done, add meatballs to sauce and simmer for 30 minutes.

THE PASTA (THE INGENUE)!!!

2 lbs of pasta (your choice of thousands!)
Large pot of water (3/4 full of water)
Salt to taste
1 T oil

1. Fill large pot 3/4 full of water; add salt and oil; bring to a boil.
2. Add pasta and stir well (to separate pasta).
3. Stir occasionally and test pasta for the firmness you prefer.
4. When done, drain pasta in collander.

You'll never see "white" spaghetti on an Italian table. The pasta and gravy are mixed well before coming to the table!

OPENING NIGHT FOR THE ULTIMATE SPAGHETTI DINNER (Scene 1: The Prologue)

I love arranging an Italian feast! I invite friends close enough to adopt the camaraderie and cooperation needed to bring the food to the table at the peak of its preparation. That kitchen cluster becomes the first course of my spaghetti dinner party—the fun of preparing the final stages of the meal itself. Guests are invited to the kitchen where an array of appetizers are already placed at their fingertips. They are asked to pour drinks and help themselves to their favorite snack (as I said earlier, people need to eat right away). And then we all share in the steps that pull the meal together. There are many tasks that can be delegated, and you can plan for them ahead of time:

• Salad needs chopping and dressing
• Garlic bread needs heating, unwrapping, and broiling to golden brown
• Meat needs segregation and assembling on platters
• Pasta needs stirring, straining, and assembly
• Candles need to be lit
• Gravy boat needs to be filled with sauce
• Cheese dish needs to be filled
• Etc., etc., etc. (as the king would say in *The King and I*)

…And so the fun continues with soothing musical accompaniment or singing if you like!

For me, the kitchen has always been the equivalent of the "wings" or backstage area of a theatre, where all the preparations are done, and props and costumes are kept and assembled in perfect order for each scene as needed. The table becomes the stage or platform upon which the drama unfolds. Each dish represents the stars and players that bring the audience the excitement and nourishment that warrant a standing ovation at the finale, while sweets and coffee are finished. At my grandma's house, the women in the family would muster in the kitchen at the precise moment that everything had to be assembled, and put onto service platters. What a parade to the table! And because there was always a short wait between courses, singers and storytellers had their chance to shine between delicious treats. How sad that today we rush through our meals together—even at banquets.

For a smooth, interactive dinner with friends, the trick is to have all the service pieces ready and tagged with notes so you can direct the traffic at all times. Here are some suggestions for managing a dinner party for eight—keeping everyone busy and aware of the timing of the "Curtain Going Up!" If you follow these steps, you'll have everything in its place at "Places!" call, when everyone is seated and ready to eat. And you and your guests will have a grand time putting the production on!

"IN THE WINGS," WITH STAGE DIRECTIONS

DINNER FOR 8: TASKS FOR YOUR GUESTS

1. Get a man to stand guard at the spaghetti sauce and stir it every five minutes to keep the meat from burning (important post!—burn the sauce and you might as well send everyone home!). To avoid this disaster, place a heat diffuser under the sauce pot and keep flame low.

2. Give someone grated cheese and an empty bowl with a small ladle. Have them fill bowl and place on the table.

3. Preheat oven to 350°. Ask someone to put wrapped garlic bread on cookie sheet and into the oven for 10 minutes while salad is being made.

4. When last guest arrives (this would be the **half-hour call**, warning everyone of curtain time), put spaghetti in boiling water with salt and oil and have someone stir it every 3 minutes. At 8 minutes, begin to test it for al dente (firmness). Just throw a piece at the wall; if it sticks, it's done and it gets a laugh every time!

5. Ask "gentleman stirrer" to lift saucepot to counter near a deep service platter.

6. Supply "gentleman stirrer" with a slotted spoon to lift meatballs out of meat sauce onto platter.

7. Meanwhile, a lady can use a fork to arrange the meats, with the meatballs curving around the edge and mix meats in center. Both gentleman and lady can then pick the best sprigs of parsley from a bag of cleaned pieces from the refrigerator and decorate the dish as they like. Gentleman places platter on table.

8. The "meatball" lady gets a gravy boat, fills it, and places it and a ladle on the table as her partner returns the pot to stove. (This is the **15-minute call**.)

9. Two ladies cut up cleaned and trimmed vegetables into large salad bowl.

Before every performance in all theatres, the stage manager calls for 30 minutes to curtain over the P.A. A 15-minute call is next, followed by a 5-minute warning and then "Places!"

10. While you mix salad and dressing together, "salad ladies" are asked to remove garlic bread from oven and slit tops of foil wrappings. Fan them open and place under low broiler for 1 1/2 minutes. Provide a lined basket and bread board and knives for cutting garlic bread as soon as it's golden brown—fast! Cut on slant and place attractively in basket and cover with napkin. Put on table. (This is the **5-minute call**.)

11. The "salad ladies" are asked to hold two salad bowls apiece while you pack them with just-mixed salad. Then ladies place each bowl to left of dinner setting and return for the last four salad bowls to be filled and placed as well.

12. Get a man to lift spaghetti strainer into sink. Get platter and cheese and someone to bring pot of sauce to it with large ladle!

13. Sprinkle platter with cheese and ladle bottom with sauce. Add half of spaghetti, smooth it to fill plate. Sprinkle again with cheese and sauce and mix well. Add remaining spaghetti, more cheese and sauce, mix spaghetti again and add a second sprinkle of cheese for beauty. Put in two serving forks and place on table.

14. Invite your cooking corps to their places at the table (**"Places" call**, of course). Give everyone permission to applaud each others' efforts—then take hands and say grace before everything gets cold!

15. Make a toast to friendship and enjoy! Buon Apetito!! Plan on accepting a lot of applause!! Then break a leg!*

*Break a leg is an expression that goes back to Shakespeare's time. It was the opening night greeting among chorus actors. The traditional Shakespearean bow was reserved for principal players only. It was done by leaning over and bending or "breaking" one knee while the other leg was extended and pointed forward. The opposite arm was lifted overhead first, and then swept back (plumed hat in hand), while the other hand rested on the hip. "Break a leg" was a way of wishing your friends a big and important role in the next play—not hoping he'd literally "break a leg"! After your friends taste your spaghetti you can take a royal Shakespearean bow and deserve it. Bravo!!!

Joey, my mother, me, and
my father after a two-hour
parade through my hometown
on "Carol Lawrence Day"
—what a thrill!

Chapter 5

The First Time Cooking for Mom

FUSSING OVER EVERYONE WAS AS NATURAL TO MY MOTHER as her sparkling dark eyes and ready laughter. Because I had been a sickly baby—with whooping cough and double pneumonia at one time, and scarlet fever, and mumps, and measles, and everything that went around—she had done more than her duty in caring for me. She never let anyone do very much for her though, and seemed always strong and capable of doing what would exhaust three other people put together.

It was a great shock to me when she was rushed to the hospital for an emergency gallbladder operation—a devastating major procedure at that time! While she was in the hospital everything fell apart at home, and as a 12-year-old I was brought to a keen appreciation of all she managed so effortlessly. Thank heaven we had lots of aunts who either sent over our hot dinner or invited us over. That was when I truly perceived how much more tasty and creative my *mom's* recipes were from all her relatives.

I missed her terribly and although I was barely 12, I was determined to show her that I too could fuss over her and show her how much I cared. I really didn't know about measurements or exactly what it was she scribbled and tested and manipulated through her magic in the kitchen. I asked my cousin Rita and my brother Joey to help me cook a dinner, and Dad agreed to drive me to the hospital to hand it to her personally.

We made a baked chicken and some simple vegetables, but managed to use every pot and pan and utensil in the house. The counters were full of dirty bowls and spills and near-disasters, but my pièce de résistance was something so far over my head that I'll never know how I had the guts to attempt it!

Somewhere in her fanciest dessert book, I saw a picture of cream puffs filled with custard and whipped cream, but best of all they had graceful necks, tails, and delicate wings, and they swam on an oval pond made of a blue mirror with real leaves at its edge.

I had just begun dancing in beautiful but painful pink satin toe shoes, and *Swan Lake* was my favorite ballet. So I tore up the kitchen trying to find a pastry tube, measured everything like a mad scientist in a laboratory, shaped all the heads and necks like a sculptress, and made a custard with the stiffest peaks of whipped cream the Midwest has ever experienced.

I stole my mother's fancy mirrored tray from under her perfume bottles on her dresser and cut some leaves from the trees in the yard. Then we wrapped everything in towels to keep the food warm and marched in triumphant glory with the first dinner I had ever cooked for the greatest culinary genius I'd ever known!

Joey and Rita walked in first and Mom oohed and aahed. But when I arrived head high and grinning over my golden tray of delicate swans, my mother burst into tears of joy and smiled through her tears, "I can't believe it. You really did that for me?!"

I'd never felt so great in all my life! When she finally stopped crying, she rang for the nurse and made her promise to take me to every room on the floor so everyone would not think she was exaggerating when she started bragging about the dinner her children had brought her. I'm afraid she did exaggerate anyway!

Mom and Dad at their thirtieth anniversary dinner.

Menu

Tomato and Mozzarella Salad
Cornish Hens with Pesto Stuffing
Baked Sweet Potatoes
Italian Green Beans
Cranberry Sauce with Nuts
Toasted Hunks of Rye Bread
Cream Puff Swans

TOMATO AND MOZZARELLA SALAD

Serves 4

> 3-4 medium tomatoes, sliced 1/4"
>   thick
> 4 fresh buffalo mozarella cheeses
> 1 bunch fresh basil
> olive oil to taste
> juice of one lemon
> Lawry's garlic salt
> salt and pepper to taste

1. Slice mozzarella and tomatoes in 1/4"
   pieces.
2. Remove stems from basil and wash
   leaves.
3. On a platter, arrange tomatoes evenly.
4. Place one slice of mozzarella on each
   tomato slice and top with a basil leaf
   (one on each slice).
5. Dribble all with oil, sprinkle with garlic
   salt, salt, pepper, and lemon juice.
   Serve.

CORNISH HENS WITH PESTO STUFFING

Serves 4

> 4 Cornish hens
> 1 small onion

PESTO STUFFING

> 3 T light oil
> 1 C brown rice
> 1/2 C chopped onion
> 1 clove garlic, minced
> 2 1/2 C chicken broth
> 1/2 C sliced celery
> 1/2 C pine nuts
> 2 T chopped, fresh basil
>   (or 2 t dried)
> 1/4 C chopped parsley
> 2 T melted margarine

1. Preheat oven to 350°.
2. Wash hens inside and out, and pat dry.
3. In large skillet, heat 2 T oil and 1 C
   brown rice. Sauté brown rice until it
   begins to darken.
4. Add onions and garlic, stir and sauté
   until transparent.
5. Add broth and celery and bring to a
   boil.
6. Cover and simmer on low heat 30 to
   40 minutes, until rice is tender.
7. In remaining oil, sauté pine nuts until
   lightly golden brown.
8. Combine nuts and rice mixture, basil
   and parsley and simmer for 3 minutes,
   uncovered.
9. Stuff cavities of hens and sew up

closure with white string using poultry needle.

10. Stuff skin at neck near breast so the bird looks really plump and round. Sew up flap of skin as well.
11. Brush all hens with melted margarine and place in covered roasting pan.
12. Chop small onion and arrange around birds in roasting pan.
13. Add 1 1/2 inches of water to pan. Cover and bake at 350° for 1 to 2 hours. When legs twist easily and are soft to the touch, remove cover and continue baking until hens are golden brown.
14. Remove hens to large serving platter and garnish with parsley.
15. Serve with light gravy

BAKED SWEET POTATOES

Serves 4

> 4 sweet potatoes or yams
> aluminum foil

1. Preheat oven to 350°.
2. Wash yams and prick each one with a fork seven or eight times, all around.
3. Wrap in aluminum foil and place in the oven (along with whatever meat is being prepared) for one hour or until they are soft and easily squeezed.
4. Remove from oven and remove foil. Place potatoes or yams on a serving plate. They may be served whole or

sliced in half lengthwise and dotted with butter and paprika.

ITALIAN GREEN BEANS

Serves 4

> 1 lb fresh Italian green beans
> (frozen may be substituted)
> 2 cloves garlic, sliced
> 2 T light oil
> 2 fresh tomatoes, peeled and
> chopped
> 1 t salt
> fresh ground pepper
> 1 t dried basil or 5 leaves fresh
> basil

1. Wash and trim tips off beans.
2. Brown garlic in light oil in skillet.
3. Add tomatoes, salt, pepper, and basil. Cook for 5 minutes.
4. Add beans and simmer 20 to 25 minutes or until tender.

CREAM PUFF SWANS

Serves 8

For Pastry

> 1/2 C butter or margarine
> 1/4 t salt
> 1 C sifted all-purpose flour
> 4 large eggs
> 1/2 C powdered sugar for
> finishing touches

For Filling

> 1 box vanilla custard mix
> 1 pt whipped cream or Cool Whip

1. Preheat oven to 400°.
2. In medium saucepan slowly bring 1 C water with butter and salt to boiling.
3. Remove from heat. With wooden spoon beat in all flour at once.
4. Return to low heat. Continue beating until mixture forms ball and leaves sides of pan.
5. Remove from heat. Beat in eggs, one at a time, beating hard after each addition until mixture is smooth.
6. Continue beating until dough is shiny and satiny and breaks into strands.
7. Divide dough in thirds.
8. Place 1/3 of dough in pastry bag.
9. Drop remaining 2/3 of dough by rounded spoonfuls onto ungreased baking sheet, 2" apart. This should make 8 puffs.
10. From pastry bag, squeeze two shapes for each puff onto additional ungreased baking sheet—one for neck and one for tail.

11. Bake puffs until puffed and brown (45-50 minutes). Puffs should sound hollow when lightly tapped with fingertip.
12. Bake shapes until golden brown—about 25 minutes.
13. Let all pastry cool completely on wire rack away from drafts.
14. Prepare filling according to box instructions. Fold in 1 C of whipped cream or Cool Whip after custard has cooled.

15. To assemble swans:
   a. Cut tops from cooled pastry puffs.
   b. Cut tops in half.

   c. Scoop out inside strands of dough to make puff hollow.
   d. Fill bottom half of puff with custard mixture.
   e. Make small hole in front of cream puff and insert back of swan's neck.

   f. Make similar hole in back of puff and insert tail.

   g. Top custard mixture with decorous amount of whipped cream or Cool Whip. Place two halves of pastry top in cream at a 45-degree angle to look like wings!

16. Sprinkle with powdered sugar.
17. Refrigerate until ready to serve.
18. Serve one per guest on a dessert plate covered with a lace doily.

For a dramatic entrance, serve swans on a mirrored tray ringed with small flowers or leaves! Add music from Swan Lake in the background!

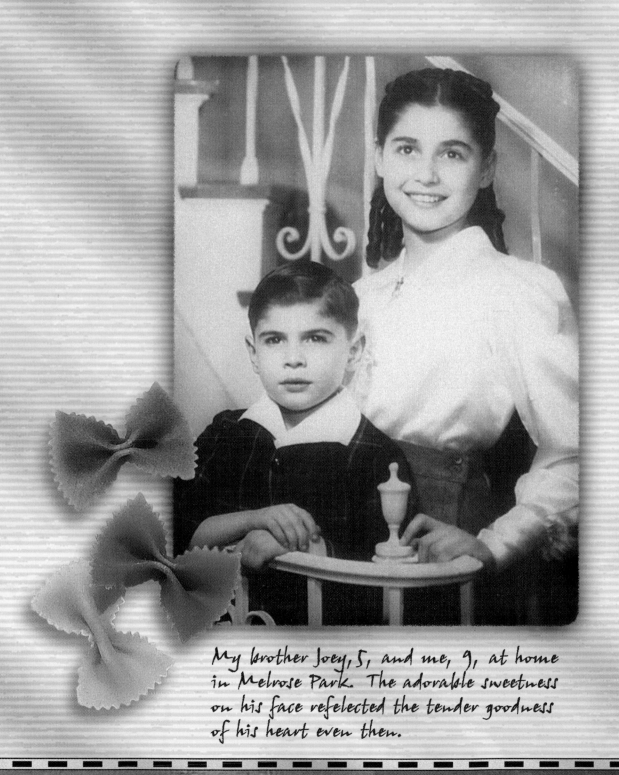

My brother Joey, 5, and me, 9, at home in Melrose Park. The adorable sweetness on his face refelected the tender goodness of his heart even then.

Chapter 6

An Evening with My Brother

*Alone
together...and
what is there to
fear... together?*

—ALONE TOGETHER

MY BROTHER JOEY IS A BRILLIANT TRIAL LAWYER. HE STANDS not terribly tall, but he's mightily respected in a toughly competitive profession—where he was named "Man of the Year" by the Illinois Bar Association and has set many precedents that dot the law books today.

In all the years of growing up together in the strict Italian discipline of hard work, good grades, and always being on our best behavior, we had lots of opportunities to take out our frustrations on each other—but amazingly enough we never had a cross word between us. It would have been understandable if Joey felt slighted by all the attention Mom gave me just getting me to lessons, rehearsals, costume fittings, and shows—and Joey was dragged along to most of them as well. He patiently accepted the hassle and has remained enthusiastic and supportive to this very day.

As youngsters we had chores to complete that helped run the house; but we found the most fun and greatest rewards in helping Mama or my aunts in the kitchen, where we always got to sample the preparations along the way. Those lessons gave us a camaraderie in the kitchen—we still love to cook together and catch up on each other's dreams. Here is a simple combination of healthy, easy, and tasty dishes that we've cooked so many times they almost come together without thinking.

CHOPPED VEGETABLE SALAD

Serves 2

> 4 carrots
> 8 radishes
> 4 stalks celery
> 4 scallions
> 1/2 head red cabbage
> 1/2 green pepper
> 1/2 sweet red pepper

1. Wash all vegetables thoroughly.
2. Slice carrots, radishes, celery, and scallions into 1/4" round pieces.
3. Slice and chop cabbage, green peppers and red peppers, into bite-size pieces.
4. Combine all vegetables in large salad bowl. With large wooden spoon mix in Joey's dressing thoroughly. Serve in individual salad bowls.

JOEY'S SPECIAL DRESSING

Serves 2

Joey is my brother and my best friend—a great treat for us is a quiet dinner where the two of us can talk. In searching for a perfect salad dressing, Joey, who also loves to cook, discovered Balsamic vinegar and sugar to taste—I added the yogurt for a creamy dressing.

> 1/2 C Balsamic vinegar
> 1/2 C low-fat plain yogurt
> 2-3 t sugar, to taste

Combine all three ingredients in small mixing bowl; with wooden spoon mix thoroughly until yogurt is smooth.

BROILED BREAST OF CHICKEN

Serves 2

> 2 full breasts of chicken (deboned)
> Lawry's garlic salt
> 2 T melted margarine
> 2 T chopped parsley
> 4 T grated parmesan cheese
> oregano and coarse pepper

1. Preheat oven to broil (500°).
2. Wash chicken breasts (remove the skin if you like). Flatten each half between two sheets of waxed paper and beat with a wooden mallet.
3. Brush all sides of meat with margarine

Chopped Vegetable Salad
Joey's Special Dressing
Broiled Breast of Chicken
Braised Carrots
French-Style Peas
Fresh Berries with Yogurt
Thin-sliced Pumpernickel Toast

and sprinkle with garlic salt.

4. Place in broiling pan under broiler until white and crisp, approximately 7 to 8 minutes.

5. Turn breasts over. Add more salt and broil 5 to 6 minutes, until fully cooked .

6. Sprinkle with cheese, oregano, and pepper to taste.

7. Return breasts to oven until cheese is golden brown. Serve.

BRAISED CARROTS

This is a truly tasty dish! The natural sweetness of the carrot is preserved by the careful light cooking. The amount will look enormous to begin with, but will reduce by 1/2 while cooking as the moisture in the carrots will be cooked away. To make this lo-cal, no-fat, merely spray pan with cooking spray, leave out butter, and follow all other directions.

3 carrots per person to be served
1 t butter or margarine per 3 carrots

1. Peel carrots and remove stem end.
2. Shred using largest opening of hand grater, or use food processor.
3. Melt butter or margarine in large skillet; add carrots.
4. Cover and steam slowly. ADD NO WATER. Carrots will cook in the butter and their own moisture. Stir frequently to prevent sticking. Braise until just tender and still firm.

FRENCH-STYLE PEAS
Serves 4

1 lb fresh peas (or 1 lb pkg frozen
early peas)
2 to 3 large lettuce leaves salt
dried basil

1. Line a saucepan with lettuce leaves so there are enough to wrap peas totally.
2. Place peas on lettuce. Sprinkle with salt and basil.
3. Fold lettuce leaves around peas to cover completely. Place lid on pot.
4. Heat 7 to 10 minutes over low heat, until tender.
5. Discard leaves. Place peas in serving dish and dot with butter or margarine.

Me, Joey, Mike, and Chris— cooking up a storm for fun in the loving kitchen!

George Burns and me backstage when we performed together at Caesar's Palace in Las Vegas. After Mostaccioli and Braccioli dinner, he regaled us with his vaudeville stories till dawn.

Chapter 7

Pasta with George

Memories,

light the corners

of my mind.

Misty water-

colored memories,

of the way

we were.

—THE WAY WE WERE

THE FIRST TIME I MET GEORGE BURNS, I FELT LIKE A DAMSEL IN distress, and he came to my rescue. He was the senior statesman of show business and had become almost a member of everyone's family after his hit TV series. His wit and spontaneous repartee were legend, but for me his greatest gift was his kind generosity toward young and frightened newcomers. I feel exceedingly privileged to have worked with him.

George came to my rescue on my opening night at the Coconut Grove of the Ambassador Hotel in Los Angeles. It was *the* place to play! It was the debut of my nightclub act on the West Coast, after having received wonderful reviews in New York City. Needless to say, it was an important engagement, and I was nervous! The first number was very fast and choreographed with two young male dancers with nary a second to focus on the audience.

We got through it, and then came my moment to say, "Hello, everybody." I gazed at a packed house and began to make out the faces of every star I had admired in the movies since I was a kid—from Cary Grant to Loretta Young to June Havoc and Fred MacMurray—and it went on! But most intimidating of all was that two inches away from me, center stage, ringside, was a table of four people who represented the royalty of theatre—Jack Benny, Mary Livingston, Gracie Allen, and George Burns.

I stared at them with a frozen sickly grin—frozen because my upper lip felt glued to my teeth, and I knew my lungs had forgotten how to breathe. It was in that split second that George Burns got to his feet, put down his cigar, winked and me, and said, "Go get 'em, kid," and started applauding.

The entire audience followed suit, standing and applauding too. My eyes filled with tears and my lungs with air, and in my laughter of relief I found the words to continue.

I've never forgotten how sensitive and resourceful George Burns was in coming to my aid. I thanked him profusely when he came backstage, not only that night but many times during the engagement when he would bring friends to see my show.

The best part of this story is that I got a chance to retell the event and thank him publicly every night when we worked together at Caesar's Palace in Las Vegas later. When I asked him if I could cook something for him, his eyes lit up. So the next night after the second show, I knocked on his dressing room door and wheeled in Mostaccioli with Braccioli, Italian salad, garlic bread, fresh fruit, and sherbet.

"Hey, kid, you weren't kiddin'!" he smiled.

It was after 2:00 A.M., but my sons, my two dancers, our conductors, and our costume people ate with George Burns. And then, like little children, we sat at his feet while he regaled us with stories of his childhood in vaudeville. It was dawn before we finally thought of sleep, and of how tired we were. It seemed, though, that George Burns never got tired!

Me, George, and Joey in George's dressing room.

Mostaccioli
Braccioli
Italian Salad
Italian Hard Rolls
Myrtle's Rice Pudding

MOSTACCIOLI AND BRACCIOLI

Serves 4

It is a fact that pasta has become the athlete's "dream-delicious" mainstay for quick energy. Perhaps that's why so many of the old "Italian" varieties are gaining in popularity! We all love to try a new twist and pasta makers have been creative for centuries! There are zitti, rigatoni, fussilli, capellini, linguine, penne, rotelli, spaghetti (of course!)—and one of my favorites, Mostaccioli!

It's fabulous with a platter of braccioli, all enhanced, of course, with the ever-present sauce!

Braccioli is one of the featured meats of spaghetti sauce—your sauce of the day. See page 43 for the basic recipe.

    3 large pieces of flank steak (butterfly cuts, so you have 6 thin pieces)
    12 cloves finely chopped garlic
    1 bunch parsley, coarsely chopped
    2 C grated parmesan
    1 C unseasoned bread crumbs
    Coarsely ground pepper to taste
    Piece of suet (2" by 4"), chopped finely
    String to tie rolled flank steak

1. Layer each ingredient in turn on the 6 pieces of meat, spreading them evenly and equally around.
2. Roll the meat jelly-roll fashion and tie firmly.
3. Braise lightly in garlic oil until brown.
4. Add the rolled steaks to your spaghetti sauce along with spare ribs, lamb shank, and other varieties of meat and cook 2 to 3 hours or until tender.
5. Make a separate platter of mostaccioli.
6. Untie and discard string from rolled steak.
7. Slice rolled flank steak crosswise (like a jelly roll) and display it in circles or around edge of platter.
8. Pile lamb, pork, and veal in center.

MYRTLE'S RICE PUDDING

    1 qt milk
    6 eggs
    1 C sugar
    pinch of salt
    1 t vanilla
    3/4 C cooked rice
    1 1/2 C dark raisins
    sprinkle nutmeg and cinnamon on top

1. Combine all ingredients and pour into greased 9" by 12" Pyrex© baking dish.
2. Place baking dish in a larger baking pan filled with 1 1/2 inches of water.
3. Bake in a 350° oven for 1/2 hour.
4. Remove and stir contents and bake again for another 1/2 hour.
5. Serve hot or cold.

To "butterfly" means to slice the slab of meat into two thin pieces so meat looks like it is split into butterfly wings.

Mostaccioli looks like this:

Ta Da!!! Here's the only thing that could stop Mickey from teasing me on stage— the promised homemade ravioli, made at a restaurant I commandeered in Houston.

Chapter 8

I Remember Mickey Rooney Ravioli

"MICKEY ROONEY RAVIOLI" MAY SOUND LIKE A NEW "IRISH" spin-off for Ragu products—but for me it conjures up one of my favorite food frolics.

When I was asked to replace Ann Miller in the very successful international tour of *Sugar Babies*, I was thrilled to be working opposite the legendary Mickey Rooney. I had only five days to learn all the tap dances, sketches, and songs. The pressure was enormous.

On opening night, I sat nervously in the dark wings, waiting for my entrance into my first big number. I was pushed in on suitcases which were to be maneuvered out on a rolling luggage cart by four tap-dancing red caps. Mickey had just finished the hotel sketch which ended with him in long red underwear. Suddenly in the dark, I heard his raspy voice whiz past me, "I'm gonna introduce you, kid. Okay?"

Then the lights came up, and he was running just in front of the careening cart and shouting at the audience, "Hey, Toronto, are you ready for her, folks? Let me hear you welcome the fabulous Carol Lawrence!" They burst into applause and screams. I broke into the biggest grin of sheer delight, and the dancers just broke up. The number never went so well! It was the perfect way to break the ice and welcome me into the fold. He even made a speech in my honor at the close of the performance, and I was overwhelmed with gratitude. I ran to his dressing room to thank him, and as I left I said, "We Italians really say 'thank you' and 'I love ya' with food. So what'll it be, Mick?"

Without a milliseconds' delay came, "Ravioli!"

"Come on, Mickey. I'm not even near a store! Gimme a break!"

He loves to tease—and even incorporated it into the performance of the "Opera Diva" sketch that ended with me fainting into the arms of three comics, him holding my right shoulder, and the others holding my hands and waist.

As I faint, the emcee yells, "Rub her wrists." The three echo, "Rub her wrists." Then follows, "Rub her elbows!" Echo, "Rub her elbows!"

But each time Mickey echoed, it would be, "Ravioli!" Soon the whole cast was in on the joke, and I had to do something quickly.

In Houston, a beautiful Victorian home had been converted into a restaurant, and my hairdresser knew the owner. We found that they were closed on our night off as well, so I rented the place. I begged all the dancers and a few showgirls to help me, and we started chopping and peeling garlic and parsley at 6 A.M. The whole cast, crew, orchestra, dressers, and hairdressers were invited. And though I only made enough ravioli for Mickey and his wife, I did make spaghetti, meatballs, salad, garlic bread, and dessert for all.

A cheery, starving Mickey Rooney ate three heaping plates of ravioli, and the Opera Diva sketch went back to the original dialogue.

Thank goodness!

Shrimp Cocktail

Ravioli

Mike's Garlic Bread

Mixed Italian Salad with Dressing

Bubbling Pastel Melon Balls

The look on Mickey Rooney's face was worth all the hours of preparation.

SHRIMP COCKTAIL

Serves 8

I always use stemmed cocktail glasses for serving this dish. The lettuce leaves line the bowl of the glass, creating a pretty setting. Slit a lemon wedge crosswise and attach it to the edge of the glass.

> 24 large, fresh shrimp (If your guests are football players, or my sons, allow double the number of shrimp per guest.)
> 1/2 onion
> 3 stalks celery
> 8 large lettuce leaves
> 8 decorative sprigs parsley
> 8 lemon wedges
> 24 crisp crackers (I prefer Ritz Crackers, which are also available in a low-fat variety.)

1. Fill 1 1/2 qt saucepan with salted water.
2. Slice onion.
3. Chop celery in 3/4" pieces.
4. Add celery and onion to salted water and boil for 5 minutes. Remove from heat and add shrimp. Cover and allow to steep for 5-7 minutes, until shrimp are pink.
5. Remove from water, shell (leaving tail intact), de-vein if necessary, and chill until time to serve.
6. To serve, place one lettuce leaf on each individual serving plate; the lettuce should line the plate, with the edges overlapping prettily. Place the serving of shrimp decoratively on the dish. Spoon approximately 2 T cocktail sauce over the shrimp. Garnish with a wedge of lemon and a sprig of parsley. Add three crisp crackers to the edge of the serving plate.

COCKTAIL SAUCE

You can use commercial cocktail sauce, which you can "doctor" to fit your own taste, or you can follow this easy recipe. The finely chopped celery is the thing that makes this cocktail sauce so special.

> 1 1/2 C ketchup
> juice of 1/2 lemon
> dash Tabasco sauce (to taste)
> dash worchestershire sauce (to taste)
> 1 t horseradish
> 1 stalk celery
> coarsely ground black pepper

1. Chop celery very fine.
2. In a medium-sized bowl mix all ingredients thoroughly. Chill well and serve.

RAVIOLI

Serves 8

For a low-fat version of ravioli, use skim milk ricotta, 6 egg whites rather than 4 eggs, and ground turkey instead of pork.

I Remember Pasta

THE RAVIOLI STUFFING

        1/4 C cooking oil
        1 1/2 lbs ground pork
        1 C parsley
        4 lbs ricotta cheese
        4 eggs
        1 C grated parmesan cheese
        salt, pepper, and sugar (to taste)

1. In a large skillet, brown pork in oil until done, breaking it in very small pieces.
2. Chop parsley, discarding all stems.
3. In a large mixing bowl, combine browned pork with ricotta, mix well.
4. In a small bowl, beat four eggs, and combine with meat and cheese mixture.
5. Add parmesan cheese and chopped parsley; mix well, adding salt, pepper, and sugar to taste.
6. Reserve in refrigerator until pasta dough is ready for filling.

THE RAVIOLI DOUGH

This is a very delicate dough and must be kneaded very smooth before resting. When it is done right it looks like shiny silk!

        2 large eggs, room temperature
        2/3 C warm water
        1 T oil
        1/2 t salt
        4 C sifted flour

1. In a very large mixing bowl, beat eggs until pale yellow.
2. Add warm water, oil, and salt, beat thoroughly.
3. Add flour, mixing well, and then remove from bowl and knead on a floured board until the dough is a very smooth texture.
4. Let stand at least one hour before rolling out, or refrigerate overnight.

ASSEMBLING THE RAVIOLI
Stuffing the Dough

Mom always made these jumbo-sized raviolis, but, of course, tiny versions are pretty and easier to handle.

1. Divide the dough into thirds.
2. On a floured board, roll each third, one at a time, into a large circle about 1/8" thick and 20" in diameter.
3. From each circle, make strips of ravioli dough 18" long and 5" wide.
4. On 1/2 of strip, the edge nearest you, drop 1 rounded tablespoon of the ricotta/meat mixture every three inches.
5. Fold dough over in half, over mounds of ricotta mixture, and press dough down in between each mound.
6. With a zigzag rolling cutter, cut equally in between mounds; pull resulting small, filled squares (ravioli) apart and press the three open edges together with the tines of a fork.

7. Pierce each mound twice with a fork to release air while cooking.

I love the fluted edge you get by pressing fork tines all around the edges—it secures the ricotta and is the first chore Nana taught my son Michael. Kids love pressing the edges and then spearing the round mound twice with a fork. What power!

COOKING AND SERVING THE RAVIOLI

Next, you will need a 3-quart kettle of boiling salted water and a serving platter.

Adding a tablespoon of cooking oil to your boiling water will keep the pasta from sticking together.

Please do not overcook! If fluted edges get too soft, they open and you have useless floating ricotta and flapping dough ... and worst of all, saddened and still-hungry guests!

8. Carefully drop raviolis into boiling, salted water and cook until tender— only 6-8 minutes; drop small scraps of dough into water so that you can test the firmness and doneness of the ravioli.
9. Remove from water with slotted spoon, or pour carefully into collander to avoid breaking—ravioli are very fragile!
10. On a large platter, spoon a layer of spaghetti sauce and sprinkle with

parmesan cheese.

11. Arrange ravioli round side up on pre-pared platter, cover with spaghetti sauce, and sprinkle with additional parmesan cheese. This dish is the same "role" played by cooked spaghetti in the "Ultimate Spaghetti Dinner" menu. The ravioli is accompanied by the regular platter of meatballs and assorted meat from the sauce. Just follow the steps to that dinner and know that this prima donna will bring down the house!

MIKE'S GARLIC BREAD
Serves 8-10
This is my son Michael's favorite garlic bread recipe, and it is delicious!

> 2 large loaves Italian bread
> 16-20 large garlic cloves
> 12 T butter
> 4 T olive oil
> 1 C grated parmesan cheese
> 2 t basil
> 2 t oregano
> 2 t salt

1. Peel and crush garlic with a garlic press; blend with butter, oil, 1 cup of cheese, basil, oregano, and salt. (This can be done a few days in advance.)
2. Slice each loaf of bread in half length-wise; spread garlic butter mixture on each half. Top with remaining cheese

For an added touch, run the bread under the broiler just before serving to toast the edges. This adds to the flavor. Be careful, though, and don't let it burn!

and bake on a foil-covered cookie sheet at 450° for 3 to 6 minutes (depending on your oven). Slice in pieces and serve.

MIXED ITALIAN SALAD (WITH DRESSING)
Serves 8

My trick when the salad is too much for a mixing bowl—I merely put all the veggies in my CLEAN kitchen sink, and mix it to my heart's content! The most fun is to ask your child to wash hands, stand on a chair and join you mixing in the sink. It's a terrific learning game!

All salad greens and vegetables except the tomatoes can be cut ahead of time and kept in the refrigerator.

1 head romaine lettuce
1/2 head iceberg lettuce
1/2 head purple cabbage
7 carrots
1 cucumber
8 radishes
2 stalks celery
1 bunch scallions
1/2 red onion
2 tomatoes

1. Wash and pat dry romaine lettuce leaves. (Romaine lettuce leaves are best dried between layers of paper towels and refrigerated until ready to mix.)
2. Wash all vegetables and drain in collander.
3. Tear lettuce and cut cabbage into chunky bite-sized pieces.
4. Peel carrots and slice in 1/4" rounds.
5. Peel cucumber, then score the length all around with the sharp tines of a large fork, this will give it a delicate edge when sliced. Slice in half lengthwise and then in 1/4" pieces.
6. Slice radishes in similar rounds.
7. Trim celery and cut in half lengthwise and then slice in 1/4" pieces.
8. Trim scallions and slice into 1/4" rounds, using as much green stem as possible.
9. Chop red onion in small pieces. Slice one round of the red onion before chopping; place single rings of onion on top of salad after mixing for color and decoration.
10. Mix all chopped vegetables well and refrigerate.
11. Just before mixing salad, cut tomatoes in chunks, easy to handle and asymmetrical. (Don't cut up the tomatoes until just before tossing. Leave them whole in a bowl where they will look beautiful until you need them.)

THE ITALIAN DRESSING

1/2 C safflower oil
4-6 cloves garlic
coarsely ground black pepper
pinch of sugar
sprinkle of dried basil

sprinkle of dried oregano

salt to taste

2 fresh lemons

1. Place all chopped vegetables from salad in a very large mixing bowl. Pour oil over vegetables.
2. Crush garlic and sprinkle on salad.
3. Sprinkle with pepper, sugar, basil, oregano, and salt.
4. Squeeze lemon over all.
5. Now is the fun! With newly washed hands, dive into the bowl and mix all seasonings through the vegetables really well.
6. Taste it and readjust to make it tangy and spicy, but not overpowering.
7. Fill chilled individual salad bowls while hands are "dirty" with salad and dressing!

Finally! Ravioli
for Mickey Rooney

BUBBLING PASTEL MELON BALLS
Serves 8

I always serve this refreshing end of the meal in my best crystal goblets. Any serving dish that is clear and lets the delightful color of this dessert shine through will complement the presentation. If you wish, you can pass a tray of biscotti with coffee or espresso with a slice of lemon peel.

1 large cantaloupe

1 medium honeydew melon

1 pt. blueberries (fresh or frozen)

1 pt. raspberries (fresh or frozen)

1 pt. lemon sherbet or sorbet

1 pt. raspberry sherbet or sorbet

2 cans chilled 7-Up©

1. Slice both melons in half and scoop out seeds. With a small melon ball maker, create as many melon balls as will allow.
2. Place a few balls of each melon at the bottom of each serving dish; sprinkle with a few blueberries and raspberries.
3. Top melons and berries with one scoop each of lemon and raspberry sherbet.
4. Add additional berries to the top of the sherbet.
5. Just before serving, pour a splash of 7-Up over each dish to make a bubbling entrance.

Pam and Scot Erdman, Mike, me, Chris, and Joey. A warm dinner with old friends where morsels and memories are savored together. Pastor Scot has been my sons' first youth minister, coach, and friend when they were only 9 and 11.

Chapter 9

A Valentine's Day Dinner

My funny
Valentine,
Sweet comic
valentine,
You make
me smile with
my heart.

—MY FUNNY VALENTINE

SOMETIMES THE NUTTIEST COMBINATION OF EVENTS GIVES birth to a recipe idea that deserves repeating and eating over and over again. So it was for me one Valentine's Day long ago. I apologize from the start, because this is not your typical romantic source for a menu on Cupid's day, but it does work—and so we won't try to fix it.

The ugly truth is that when my sons were seven or eight, they became enthralled with wrestling. Being totally ignorant of the sport, and knowing there was no such program at their school, I inquired at the local YMCA, where they had enjoyed many sports before. Indeed, there was a class after school, and we immediately enrolled. They loved it and rolled all over the mats, "pinning" each other and having a ball.

Since I was locked into waiting two hours for them twice a week, I began scanning the bulletin board for something for mom to wrestle with. It was absolutely perfect timing! A new class in sculpting had just begun, and I had always yearned to try that magnificent art. So I signed up and fell in love with clay. Everything I touched screamed to be molded into a never-before-experienced shape.

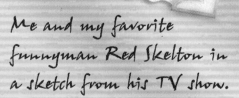

Me and my favorite funnyman Red Skelton in a sketch from his TV show.

A surprise valentine for a child's lunch could be a sandwich made with whole wheat bread cut in the shape of an angel (from a Christmas cookie cutter) and stuck together with peanut butter and red cherry jam. Use maraschino cherries for buttons and halved cherries for eyes and mouth and a small white paper doily for a halo! A sweet cheery, cherry reminder you cared enough to fuss a bit!

I filled my class with weird animal figures and even found new recipes for Jello concoctions.

Then one afternoon at the Y, I realized it was St. Valentine's Day, and I hadn't planned anything to celebrate it. The boys and I decided the three of us would have a party and build something together. We raced to the store for a meal that we could make fast because we were hungry. One of their all-time favorites was and still is meat loaf. That was a fast order, but even as I picked up the ground meat in my hands, I could feel its softness, its compliance—its moldability! Michelangelo genius struck! I could see it, as clear as the "Pieta"—I would fashion this lowly ground meat into the most beautiful heart any Romeo could wish for. My fingers were itching to start as I raced through all the aisles necessary for my artistic achievement. I would prepare only red-dominated dishes, and as I explained my plans to Chris and Mike they giggled, agreeing to help. We got so caught up with the spirit of fun, that as usual we broke into song, and had to give credit where it belonged—to the YMCA. All the way home in the car we laughed our way through the familiar Village People refrain, "YMCA…Yes, we're talkin' 'bout the YMCA…"

Here are the recipes we created; and even today we keep up the romantic menu and remember wrestling and sculpting and heart-shaped meat loaf…and laugh.

> *Heart-Shaped Meat Loaf with*
> *Carved Carrot Arrow*
>
> *Pasta with Aglia E Olio*
>
> *Red on Red on Red Salad*
>
> *Boiled Beets and Red Onion*
> *with Oregano*
>
> *Heart-Shaped Baking*
> *Powder Biscuits*
>
> *Cherry Tarts with Ice Cream*
> *and Hot Strawberry Topping*
>
> *Sparkling Red Cider*

HEART-SHAPED MEAT LOAF WITH CARVED CARROT ARROW

Serves 6

    1 1/2 lb ground beef
    1 1/2 lb ground pork
    1 C bread crumbs (plain)
    3/4 C grated parmesan
    3/4 C onions, finely chopped
    5 cloves garlic, finely minced
    3/4 C ketchup
    3/4 C minced parsley
    3 eggs beaten
    3 slices bacon
    1/2 C ketchup for garnish

1. Mix ground meats, bread crumbs, and parmesan together thoroughly.
2. Chop onion and garlic.
3. Mix all ingredients in large bowl (using hands, mix well).
4. Shape loaf in a heart.
5. Place in large roasting pan with cover.
6. Coat loaf with ketchup, and decorate with bacon, outlining shape of loaf. Cut one slice of bacon in half to trim point of heart as illustrated.
7. Cover bottom of roasting pan with 1/2" water.
8. Cover and bake at 350° for one hour.
9. Remove cover and brown for 5 minutes.
10. Remove to platter and garnish with parsley around bottom edge. Use carrot arrow for trim (see following instructions).

VALENTINE MEAT LOAF CARROT TRIM

Use a fresh carrot, leaving some leaves on the end if possible. These leaves become "feathers." Cut carrot in half; carve arrowhead shape into one end. Insert each half into meat loaf on the diagonal to resemble arrow piercing heart.

For an elaborate Valentine look, ring edge of meat loaf with tiny pearl onions atop red leaf lettuce ruffle.

PASTA AGLIA E OLIO

Serves 4

    1 lb. spinach or plain fettucine
    8-10 cloves garlic, sliced
    1/2 C virgin olive oil
    3/4 C coarsely chopped walnuts or almonds
    1 C grated Romano cheese
    1/4 C chopped parsely
    black pepper to taste

1. In a skillet brown sliced garlic until golden.
2. Remove pan from heat and toss walnuts or almonds until well coated.

To give Pasta Aglia E Olio an authentic Italian taste, sprinkle with crushed red pepper. This becomes "Pasta Aglio Peperoncino"!

It's really easy to make heart-shaped low-fat pancakes using cookie cutters. Add red crab apples on the side, strawberries and whipped (low-fat) cream as topping, and red-hot hearts as decorations in the cream. A shortcut would be to pop low-fat frozen pancakes in the microwave and then cut heart shapes and cube the leftover scraps to add to whipped cream and red hots! Fast and easy—I won't tell.

(Do *not* cook walnuts because they will turn black!)

3. Boil fettucine in salted water until cooked.
4. Drain water and return fettucine to same hot pot.
5. Pour oil mixture over pasta, add parsley, cheese, and pepper. Mix well and turn onto a serving bowl.
6. Sprinkle with a little more cheese and enjoy!

RED ON RED ON RED SALAD
Serves 4-6

> 1 small head red cabbage
> 1 large red onion
> 1 bunch of radishes, sliced
> 1 pt cherry tomatoes

Italian vinaigrette dressing
sprinkling of oregano
parsley for garnish

1. Chop cabbage in 1" bite-size pieces.
2. Cut onions into rings, then in half, so they maintain a curve.
3. Cut cherry tomatoes in half.
4. Toss all vegetables together with dressing, sprinkle with oregano.
5. Garnish with parsley, and serve in glass salad bowl or on individual dishes.

BEETS AND RED ONIONS
Serves 4

> 16-20 small, fresh beets
> 1 medium red onion, sliced in half lengthwise and then in thin rings

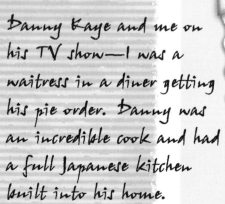

Danny Kaye and me on his TV show—I was a waitress in a diner getting his pie order. Danny was an incredible cook and had a full Japanese kitchen built into his home.

3 T light oil

oregano to taste

salt and pepper to taste

1. Trim beets, wash and boil in salted water until a fork can pierce them easily.
2. Drain and place in bowl.
3. Add sliced onion, oregano, oil, salt, and pepper.
4. This becomes a salad when chilled and is very tasty after refrigerated overnight.

HEART-SHAPED BAKING POWDER BISCUITS

Makes 8 biscuits

2 C sifted all-purpose flour

3 T baking powder

1 t salt

1/3 C shortening

about 3/4 C milk

1. Sift flour with baking powder and salt in medium mixing bowl.
2. Cut shortening into flour mixture using pastry blender or two knives, until mixture resembles coarse cornmeal.
3. Make a well in the center. Pour in 2/3 cup milk all at once. Stir quickly with a fork. If mixture seems dry, add a little more milk, to form dough just moist enough to leave side of bowl and form ball (batter should not be wet).
4. Turn out dough onto lightly floured breadboard to knead. Knead ten times: Gently pick up dough from side away from you, fold over toward you, and press lightly with palm of hand—repeat.
5. Gently roll out dough from center to 1/2" – 3/4" thickness.
6. With floured heart-shaped cookie cutter, cut straight down into dough, being careful not to twist cutter.
7. Place biscuits onto ungreased cookie sheet; bake 12 to 15 minutes in oven that has been preheated to 450°.

Johnny Carson and me. He insisted on no physical rehearsal, so all the real spontaneity of his brilliant humor was fresh for air time. I once got him to throw pizza dough on camera—and he was hysterical!

A Healing Meal

WHEN I LOOK BACK ON MY MOST CHERISHED MEMORIES, I FIND them stretching out in my mind like telephone poles along the highway of my life. In the rolling terrain of those growing-up years and early adulthood, each treasured memory is like a landmark capturing the peaks of excitement and joy of family life as well as the sometimes grueling and pressured days of ordinary living. I always find that among the memories is a table, topped with home-cooked treasures. How food has coated our senses from earliest remembrance!

I was six years old when we learned that I was to be quarantined in my own home for many months because I had a very contagious case of scarlet fever. Only my mama could be present to care for me. My dear father and little brother, on the other hand, had to stay with relatives to avoid contamination.

I was so weak with fever during the long days that no matter what delectable morsel my mama placed before me, it held no interest whatsoever. But then my mama tried my grandmother's stracciatelli soup. It was the only thing I couldn't resist!

Nana would brave exposure to the fever in order to bring a pot of freshly prepared soup to my mama for passing along to me. It was so tasty—light, easy to digest, and full of healing and nourishing substance. Her sunny spirit was somehow contained in that delicious broth for it was, I'm convinced, the magic ingredient that turned me back toward health—a true homeopathic remedy. I called it Nana's "Italian Penicillin."

Stracciatelli (Italian Penicillin) Chicken Soup Extraordinaire!

Serves 6

Mama's Version

   1 large chicken, cut into pieces

   8 medium carrots, scraped and sliced
      into nickel-sized rounds

   6 large stalks celery with leaves,
      sliced 1/4" thick

   3 lg. yellow onions, chopped

   1 bunch parsley, coarsely chopped

   1 bunch scallions with greens,
      sliced like carrots

   4 T dried basil (fresh, 4 leaves,
      torn in pieces)

   salt and pepper to taste

   2 large cubes chicken boullion

   large stock pot 3/4 full of water

Step #1

1. Add chicken (including innards and neck) to boiling, salted water. Return to boil.
2. Remove dark residue with tea strainer, and wipe sides of pan above surface with a paper towel.
3. Simmer 20 minutes.
4. Add remaining ingredients and simmer 10-15 minutes, or until carrots are cooked but still firm.
5. Remove from heat and take chicken out to cool.
6. Refrigerate soup until all the fat congeals on the surface. Remove and discard fat (no more cholesterol!).

7. When the chicken is cool, remove skin and debone. Reserve a breast and thighs for sandwiches or a cold entree.
8. Cut meat into small bite-sized pieces, set aside.

Step #2

   4 eggs

   1/4 C cream

   1/4 C semolina flour

   1 C parmesan cheese grated

My Modifications to Step #2

(for obvious reasons)

The changes are merely to reduce the fat content and really do not impair the delicious combination of ingredients. I suggest you never try Nana's recipe or you will be spoiled! At first taste, my version is fantastic.

   6 egg whites

   1/4 C lowfat milk

   3/4 C parmesan cheese

1. Combine all ingredients in bowl and beat with a whisk until smooth.
2. Bring stock to a fast boil and add mixture all at once to soup.
3. Continue to stir with large fork until egg mixture puffs up (about 3-4 minutes).
4. Add shredded chicken and serve.

Rice Pilaf

Serves 4

   3 T margarine

   1 medium onion, finely chopped

   1/2 t salt

Stracciatelli

Rice Pilaf

Garlic Spinach

Cucumber Salad

Poppy Seed Rolls

Espresso Jello

---

1 C rice (preferably brown)
1 C water
1/4 C chopped parsley

1. Saute onion in skillet until transparent.
2. Add rice, salt, and water; stir well; bring to boil.
3. Reduce heat and simmer for 40 minutes or until rice is tender.
4. Remove to serving dish and garnish with parsley.

GARLIC SPINACH
Serves 4

    3-4 large bundles fresh spinach
    8-10 cloves garlic
    1/2 C light oil
    2 dried Melrose Park peppers broken in pieces
    crushed red peppers (optional)
    salt and pepper

1. Wash and trim spinach stems.
2. Slice garlic lengthwise and brown in oil in large skillet.
3. Remove garlic and set aside.
4. Add spinach, pack down, cover and sauté until cooked.
5. Add peppers or small amount of crushed red peppers and garlic.
6. Mix well, add salt and pepper to taste.

CUCUMBER SALAD
Serves 6 to 8

    4 medium cucumbers
    1 T plus 2 t salt

    1 1/2 C non-fat plain yogurt
    1/4 C cider vinegar
    1 1/2 t sugar
    1 t celery seed
    1/4 C chopped chives
    1/2 C chopped fresh dill
    paprika

1. Peel cucumbers and slice thinly.
2. Toss the slices in a bowl with 1 T salt.
3. Cover with a plate and weight down to press out the juices.
4. Refrigerate for 2 or 3 hours.
5. Mix the yogurt, vinegar, remaining salt, sugar, celery seed, and chopped chives.
6. Drain the cucumbers and place in a serving bowl.
7. Reserving a good handful of the chopped dill, add the rest of the dill and toss with the cucumbers.
8. Pour sauce over and toss again. Garnish the top with a good sprinkling of paprika and the reserved handful of dill.
9. Chill before serving.

POPPY SEED ROLLS
Serves 8-10

This roll is one of my most vivid memories of treats made by my Aunt Teresa; I remember the poppy seeds being sweet and crunchy and that I had never seen a food that was black and white before. This kind of sweet bread can be filled with many other things besides poppy seeds, and I have included a few examples.

A coleslaw slicer is handy for slicing cucmbers.

Basic Sweet Dough

1/4 C milk
1/4 C sugar
1/2 t salt
3 T butter or margarine
1/4 C warm water
1 pkg active dry yeast
1 egg beaten
2 1/2 C sifted all purpose flour
1 egg beaten and thinned with water,
   for glaze

1. In small saucepan, heat milk just until bubbles form around edge of pan; remove from heat.
2. Add sugar, salt, and butter, and stir until butter is melted. Let cool to lukewarm.
3. Dissolve yeast in warm water in large mixing bowl. (Follow directions on yeast package carefully; water must not be too warm.)
4. Stir in milk mixture, and add beaten egg and 1 1/2 C flour; beat with wooden spoon until smooth; add rest of flour and beat until dough is smooth and leaves sides of bowl. (This may require mixing with your hands, as dough is stiff. This is one of the pleasures of baking bread—it is a very "hands on" experience, unless you have a dough hook or a bread machine.)
5. Turn out dough on lightly floured bread board or other flat surface; knead until dough is satiny and elastic and blisters appear on surface. (See kneading instruc-

tions in baking powder biscuit recipe, p. 75.)
6. Place in lightly greased large bowl; turn so all sides are greased. Cover with warm, damp towel and let rise in warm place (85°), free from drafts, until double in bulk (about 1–1 1/2 hours). (I use the top of the stove, under the stove light to encourage the dough to rise quickly.)
7. When dough has doubled in bulk, punch down with fist; turn out onto lightly floured bread board or pastry cloth. Knead 10-12 times.
8. Roll out dough into rectangle about 16" by 10"; dough should be about 3/8" thick.
9. Fill with poppy seed filling (or other filling), spreading filling to 1/2" from edge of dough.
10. Roll filled rectangle like a jelly roll—you may leave the roll long, in which case fold under the ends to seal the roll; you may also roll the length into a snail shape, tucking the end under.
11. Place on a greased cookie sheet, and cover with warm, damp towel, and let rise again in warm place, until double in bulk (this takes about 1/2 hour).
12. When the dough has risen the second time, brush bread with a beaten egg that has been thinned with water, sprinkle with poppy seeds and sugar and bake in 325° oven for 30-35 minutes, or until the loaf is golden brown and sounds hollow when tapped. Remove from oven, cool slightly and eat.

These rolls served warm right out of the oven are fabulous!

POPPY SEED FILLING

 1 1/2 C poppy seeds, crushed
 1 C milk
 3/4 C sugar
 2 T butter or margarine

1. Combine all ingredients in saucepan.
2. Cook until mixture is thick, but still moist—
   it should achieve a doughlike consistency. If
   it is too moist, it will penetrate the walls of
   the bread and burn in the oven.

ALMOND SUGAR FILLING

 1 roll almond paste
 1/4 C sugar
 3 T butter or margarine

1. Combine all ingredients in mixing bowl,
   creaming until smooth.
2. Spread on rolled-out dough.
3. Roll dough into snail shape.
4. Decorate this one with beaten egg
   mixture, sliced almonds, and a sprinkling
   of sugar.

CINNAMON RAISIN FILLING

 2 C dark brown sugar
 1 T cinnamon
 1/2 C milk
 1/4 t salt
 2 T butter
 1 t vanilla
 1 C raisins
 1 C walnuts (optional)

1. Combine sugar, cinnamon, milk, salt, and
   butter in medium saucepan; bring to boil,
   stirring constantly until butter is melted.
2. Boil slowly, stirring often, until mixture
   forms a very soft ball in cold water.
3. Remove from heat and stir in raisins and
   walnuts.
4. Cool until thick; spread on rolled-out
   dough.
5. Roll dough into long roll; let rise again.
6. Brush this one with egg mixture, sprinkle
   with sugar, and dot with raisins and nuts.
7. Extra filling may be made to use as a
   frosting on this cinnamon roll; remove
   roll from oven when done and frost
   immediately while still very hot.

ESPRESSO JELLO
Serves 6

 2 envelopes unflavored gelatin
 1/2 C brandy
 3 C freshly made hot Italian or
   French coffee (or very
   strong regular coffee)
 3 T sugar
 lightly sweetened whipped cream

1. Sprinkle gelatin over brandy and let soften
   for 10 minutes.
2. Sweeten coffee with sugar.
3. Mix with gelatin and stir until gelatin is
   completely dissolved.
4. Pour into 6 crystal goblets or glass dessert
   dishes and chill until set.
5. Top with lightly sweetened whipped cream.

Chapter 11

Lasagna for Ol' Blue Eyes

ONE OF THE AXIOMS OF SHOW BUSINESS IS THAT THE BIGGER and more famous a star is, the nicer that real person inside remains. Nothing could be truer, thank goodness. Because I've been blessed by having worked with giants like Bob Hope, Frank Sinatra, Gene Kelly, Maurice Chavalier, Bing Crosby, Danny Kaye, Red Skelton, and George Burns, to name a few, I want to assuage the myth that celebrities don't react with genuine appreciation to homemade spaghetti. Really, they're no different than you or I.

The first time I took on the responsibility of co-hosting a telethon for children with cerebral palsy, I was excited, thrilled, and determined to make it a rip-roaring success. I sent personally written requests to every celebrity friend I knew to make a guest appearance on it—even the so-called unattainable ones (stars who sent generous checks but had declined a personal appearance).

At the top of that list was Frank Sinatra—but did that stop me? No! I wrote the most unabashed Italian plea since Palgiacci's tearful aria right to Blue Eyes himself. And waited. All of my buddies who were in town agreed to come on and we were encouraged.

Two days before the event, I went on the "Tonight Show" to plug the telethon and during the rehearsals got a phone call that pulled me off the stage. It was him!

"Who, him?"

"Himself, Frank!"

He wanted to accept and make sure I could announce it that evening to get more people tuned to the telethon. He is not only talented but smart too! I was ecstatic and promised him a special dish—his favorite, lasagna!

The finale of our whole show was his appearance—the studio was crammed with screaming fans, the building surrounded with security guards and electricity ran through our veins as he made his entrance.

He had warned us that he wouldn't be able to perform because his musicians were at that moment rehearsing in a ballroom in town for a benefit stint later that night. But he had prepared a beautiful pitch for raising money and brought his own cue cards so as to get it just right.

He made an eloquent plea and the phones rang off the wall. Then my very Italian conductor, Joe Parnello (also Frank's conductor at times!) called to him from the piano, "Come on, Frank. Sing something."

"I don't have my music. You know that, Joe," Frank spoke through clenched teeth.

"I'll play for you from memory. How about..." and he fingered "The way you wear your hat..."

Frank grinned and shook his head in surrender. He quickly changed keys and said, "Do it in this key. It's better for Carol."

"Me?" I blinked. "I don't even know the words."

"Don't worry, kid. I'll feed 'em to you!"

And we began our duet of "They Can't Take That Away from Me" in front of the world, and he never let me down or missed a chance to cue in the right word when I looked shaky. He even harmonized the ending, and we got a standing, cheering ovation.

But the kindest and most generous gesture came as he was walking off camera. We called for a tote board and we were $3,000 from the all-time record. He grabbed the floor manager's arm and whispered in his ear and left the studio.

Frank Sinatra had said, "Tell her I'm writing a check for $10,000, so it's over the record for sure!"

I couldn't believe my ears. When the final count was taken, we were many thousands over our wildest hopes and a new milestone was accomplished—more stars than ever were helping charities with their fundraising needs!

I called the next morning and got Frank's personal secretary, Dorothy. I thanked her and established where the "drop-off" would be for the lasagna. Then the following Saturday in Las Vegas, and right on time, I carried the largest pan I owned, chock-full of a mozzarella, ricotta, baby meatball lasagna, piping hot, to his dressing room with a note even more passionately Italian—full of "Une mille grazie!" (a thousand thanks). It was just a downpayment—debts like this are never paid in full.

LASAGNA

Serves 8 to 10

> The sauce is the basic Spaghetti Sauce except for an additional amount of ground beef and pork. This is made into tiny meatballs approximately 1" in diameter and cooked separately and placed into their own pan of sauce and simmered for 15 minutes to assimilate the taste of the sauce. These are worked into the layers of lasagna!

2 lbs lasagna pasta
3 lbs ground beef and pork mixed
4 lbs ricotta
2 eggs, beaten
2 T sugar
1 t salt
1/2 t pepper
1/2 C chopped parsley
3 lbs. mozzarella (shredded)
3 C grated parmesan cheese
3 T olive oil

1. Boil pasta in salted water with 3 T olive oil; stir often to keep pasta separated. Boil until just tender to the bite—it will continue to bake for one hour.
2. Mix ricotta with beaten eggs, sugar, salt, pepper, and parsley until smooth.
3. Drain pasta and put in same pot with cold water so pieces are separated and whole.
4. In large rectangular baking dish (approximately 3 1/2" to 4" deep) pour a ladle of spaghetti sauce and spread on bottom of pan. Sprinkle with parmesan cheese.
5. Layer pasta evenly to form a complete cover for bottom of pan.
6. Space tiny meatballs in rows of three, across width of pan, and alternate spacing so that meatballs are evenly spaced in each layer. Use approximately 20-25 meatballs per layer—depending on depth and size of pan. You'll need 2 or 3 layers and from 50 to 75 meatballs—probably 3 lbs. of ground meat will be needed.
7. In between meatballs drop spoonfuls of ricotta mixture and spread as evenly as possible throughout space left in layer.
8. Sprinkle a liberal amount of mozzarella over all.
9. Spoon spaghetti sauce evenly over all.
10. Sprinkle with parmesan cheese.
11. Begin another layer of pasta and repeat steps 6-10.
12. Finish by layering pasta on top of sauce in as smooth a layer as possible (always reserve your best, unbroken pieces of pasta for this layer). Sprinkle with mozzarella, an even covering of sauce, and a last sprinkle of parmesan cheese.
13. Cover tightly over last layer, allowing a bit of space above sauce so when you remove it the cheese and sauce will not adhere to it.
14. Place lasagna on a cookie sheet covered with aluminum foil to catch any dripping while baking, and place in a 350° oven for one hour.
15. Remove and place on cooling rack for 45 minutes to 1 hour before uncovering and serving.
16. To serve, cut into squares 3" x 3" or as much as a hungry guest can handle. (Don't make them too big because it is a very filling dish!)

When making lasagna, I just figure an extra three pounds of meatball recipe, and keep them separated from the rest of the meats in their own saucepan of gravy.

(left to right) Jay and Michael Laraia, my father, my
mother, my niece Kim, me (holding my Yorkshire
puppy), Michael, Mary Lou, and my brother, Joey. A
holiday portrait (Chris must be taking the picture).

Chapter 12

The Traditional Italian Christmas Eve

WHEN CHILDHOOD MEMORIES ARE PASSED DOWN AS FAMILY traditions, a calming glow deep inside reminds us that all the efforts are well worth it! Such is the case for me at every authentic Italian Christmas Eve party.

I need to preface the presentation of a Christmas Eve menu with an explanation that old world Italy forbade the eating of meat on the eve of our Lord's birth. He was made flesh and therefore none would be eaten that day in deference to Him. Hence, the challenge was to invent extravagantly delicious dishes from fish, vegetables, and fruit—and these recipes were reserved for *this* day only.

At our home, my mother's preparations began weeks in advance—canning peppers in vinegar that were filled with ground figs, nuts, and sweets and spices, baked but served *cold*. There would be artichokes, crammed full of grated cheese, breadcrumbs, raisins, garlic and sprinkled with oil, pepper, parsley and then steamed. Salads included oranges, broccoli with garlic, anise, chopped fruit, nuts in Jello, salads with layers of molded cheese too, and cold lemon fish salad of many varieties with pimento, olives and celery. The appetizers included iced clams and oysters on the half shell, shelled shrimp and spicy cocktail sauce, sautéed smelts, deep fried calamari (squid)—piping hot and served in the kitchen as you helped turn them out and sprinkled them with pepper.

The entrees consisted of pasta with red calamari gravy, scampi in a parsleyed garlic butter sauce, linguini with white clam sauce or pesto, sizzling breaded and sautéed broccoli, and steamed king crab legs with drawn butter.

The finale of desserts filled our whole buffet and looked like a three-act ballet choreographed by the sugar plum fairy! Glistening decorations topped the cookies in the shapes of snowmen, angels, drums, trees, Santas, and bells. There were pecan crescents dipped in powdered sugar, kolaches (stars filled with jam), cherry topped "chews" rolled in pecans, plump ovals studded with pinenuts, praline pumpkin pie, caramelized tapioca pudding, and blarney stones made from angel food cake squares frosted and rolled in peanut crumbs!

My marvelous brother, Joey, and I keep as much of this heirloom of delicious excess alive each year by coming together with as many loved ones who are patient enough to share the load of recreating our fondest memories of love and good cheer.

Actually, we had a commemorative show taped on the Trinity Broadcast Network, as part of my regular shows there. (We did several holiday specials.) It seemed perfect to invite Joey on for the Christmas Eve show in order to authenticate the Italian buffet. It was a whirlwind of endless calculating, chopping, cleaning, and cooking. Thank heavens we had my sons, Chris and Mike, to help as well. We were lugging all the pots, bowls, platters, strainers, spoons, and spatulas we could find at home and then transporting them two hours by car to the studio! For television you need to show the individual ingredients as well as each step of preparation; and of course the finished products provide a magical ending. Setting all that up should have required a staff of forty, and we were only four! But with the help of the Lord, we got it together and it was the show for which we got the most mail and the most requests for recipes!

No one lost their cool and the crew were ecstatic when the shoot was over and they could dive into that colorful table of love! I urge you to sample a few dishes and join the clan—Italian, that is!

Italian Stuffed Artichokes
Lemon Fish Salad
Iced Clams and Oysters
Orange Salad
Broccoli Salad with Garlic
Breaded Broccoli
Spaghetti with Calamari Sauce
Deep Fried Calamari
Smelts
Steamed King Crab Legs
Scampi in Garlic and Parsley Sauce
Linguini in White Clam Sauce (see page 30)
Candied Yams
Stuffed Vinegar Peppers
Sugar Cookies
Apple Cake with Whipped Cream
Caramelized Tapioca
Blarney Stones
Kolaches—Jam Stars
Praline-Pumpkin Pie

ITALIAN STUFFED ARTICHOKES

Serves 6

> 6 artichokes
> 1/2 cup plain bread crumbs
> 1 cup grated parmesan cheese
> 18 garlic cloves, sliced
> 1-2 cups raisins (dark)
> 1/4 cup finely chopped parsley
> pepper to taste
> safflower oil to taste
> water, enough to steam for 1 hour

1. Prepare artichokes by cutting off stems at base even with bottom leaves so it stands up easily.
2. Cut off tops and snip off thorns and tips of each leaf.
3. Spread artichoke open and wash well.
4. Slice peeled garlic cloves thinly (approximately 3 or 4 per artichoke or to taste).
5. Slip garlic slices deep in between leaves evenly distributed all around.
6. Evenly distribute raisins in between leaves so flower opens even more.
7. Mix bread crumbs and cheese together in large bowl.
8. Hold artichoke over bowl and fill with cheese mixture stuffing and spreading leaves repeatedly.
9. Place artichokes in large roasting pan with cover.
10. Sprinkle each with safflower oil (or Wesson) so top is moist.
11. Pour 1 1/2" of water into bottom of pan and liberally pepper each artichoke.
12. Top each with a pinch of finely chopped parsley.
13. Cover and place on 2 burners on stove (or in oven at 400°).
14. Bring to a boil and then reduce heat to a simmer for at least one hour, or until you can remove a large leaf easily from base of artichoke.
15. Baste with hot water frequently and add a few drops of oil to each after 1/2 hour.
16. Place a pretty plate in between each pair of guests at the table, so they can put discarded leaves on them.
17. Serve hot or cold and enjoy!

LEMON FISH SALAD

Serves 12-16

Make this fish salad either early in the day or the day before so that all the flavors of the variety of fish and spices have time to marinate. This dish heads off the traditional Christmas Eve buffet and should be just a small, cool taste contrast to the other hot, crisp items on the table.

> 4-6 oz cans conch (scungile)
>   or 1 1/2 lb Monk fish, or
>   any fish that does not
>   flake
> 3 lb calamari (squid)
> 1 1/2 lb cooked small shrimp
> 1/2 lb lobster or fake crab (pre-cooked)
> 1/2 lb white fish
> 4-5 stalks celery, chopped
> 2 small cans pimento
> 1/2 lb black olives (dried Italian
>   style)
> 10-12 cloves garlic, minced
> garlic powder to taste
> 6-7 lemons

1. Clean conch, rinsing well in cold water and cut into bite-size pieces.

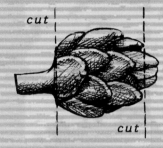

cut

cut

Be sure to maintain enough water in pan to keep steaming. Water can evaporate and burn artichokes easily, so be watchful.

2. Clean squid well, removing as much skin as possible and cut into bite-size pieces. This is a real labor of love, and I suggest having a partner you love shiver beside you and talk to you, because it will take a couple of hours with hands in cold, running water to strip the white meat from the skin.
3. Boil squid, monk, white fish, shrimp—each separately, each just until they turn white and are done. Reserve.
4. Chop celery into small pieces.
5. Chop pimento in similarly sized pieces.
6. Combine all fishes (but white fish) in large bowl with pimento, olives, celery, salt, pepper, and garlic—sprinkle with the juice of 5 lemons.
7. Fold ingredients together gently so all spices are well distributed. Adjust taste and add white fish, trying to maintain pieces intact. Be gentle.
8. Cover and refrigerate for at least one hour, preferably overnight.
9. Before serving, readjust garlic and lemon proportions with garlic powder and more lemon juice.
10. Serve cold with hot garlic toast!

ICED CLAMS AND OYSTERS
Serves 8-12

> 40 clams
> 40 oysters
> crushed ice
> 8-10 lemons
> Tabasco sauce
> cocktail sauce
> horseradish

1. Scrub clams and oysters with cold water.
2. Carefully wedge an oyster shucking knife between side of shell and pry open. Only a strong hand and careful practice will work. (This is my brother Joey's job! I relinquished it after bleeding one day from a nasty gash when the knife slipped!)
3. Once the oyster is open, loosen it completely from its shell, disengage the empty half of shell and discard. Rinse oyster again and return to half shell.
4. Repeat opening process with clams.
5. Keep opened clams and oysters in refrigerator 'til ready to serve.
6. Place a layer of crushed ice on 2 serving platters or trays and arrange clams on one and oysters on the other.
7. Cut 1/2" wedges of lemon. Add sprigs of parsley and arrange around the edge of trays.
8. Place 2 bowls of cocktail sauce with several service spoons in them near trays, along with 3 small bottles of Tabasco, and a bowl of horseradish with two spoons in it.
9. Let everyone help themselves and add the sauce and condiment they prefer.

ORANGE SALAD
Serves 4

This sparkling colored dish allows a person to cleanse the palate between the numerous spicy dishes that array the special buffet.

> 3 large Sunkist eating oranges
> scant dribble of oil
> pepper
> parsley for garnish

1. Slice oranges 3/8" thick (remove and discard "stem" ends).

2. Arrange slices side by side on a serving plate.
3. Using scant amount of oil, dribble evenly on oranges.
4. Sprinkle with finely ground black pepper.
5. Garnish with parsley.

BROCCOLI SALAD WITH GARLIC
Serves 8-10

>   large bunch broccoli
>   8 cloves garlic
>   3/4 C light oil
>   juice of one large lemon
>   (or to taste)
>   salt and pepper

1. Wash broccoli and trim excess leaves from stalks and slice lengthwise.
2. Boil until firm, yet tender enough to pierce with a fork.
3. Drain and refrigerate until cooled.
4. Mix a dressing by crushing garlic and blending with oil and lemon.
5. Salt and pepper to taste.
6. Arrange cooled broccoli on platter and dribble with dressing. Refrigerate and serve cold.

BREADED BROCCOLI
Serves 8-10

This is the last dish to be prepared along with hot smelts and calamari.

>   1 bunch broccoli
>   3 eggs
>   1 C seasoned Italian breadcrumbs
>   3/4 C light oil
>   6 cloves garlic
>   salt and pepper

1. Wash and parboil broccoli as directed in Broccoli Salad (above).
2. Slice garlic lengthwise, brown in oil in skillet, remove and set aside.
3. Beat 3 eggs in a shallow bowl and place breadcrumbs in another bowl.
4. Dip parboiled broccoli in eggs and immediately roll in seasoned bread crumbs so each piece is coated with batter.
5. Sauté broccoli in hot garlic oil until crisp and golden brown on each side. Drain on paper towels. Salt and pepper to taste and serve immediately.

SPAGHETTI WITH CALAMARI SAUCE
Serves 8-10

This can be done the night before and warmed carefully. Do not overcook, as squid will toughen.

>   1/2 C light oil
>   2 lb squid (calamari)
>   3-4 cloves garlic (sliced
>   lengthwise)
>   2 12 oz cans tomato paste
>   1 28 oz can pureed tomatoes
>   4 1/2 C water
>   salt and pepper to taste
>   1/4 C chopped parsley
>   3-4 fresh basil leaves, or 1/8 t
>   dried basil
>   1/4 C parmesan cheese

1. In large saucepan, brown sliced garlic and reserve.
2. Cut squid with kitchen shears to remove all inside cartilage and internal organs, washing squid and storing in cold water. (These are really messy fish, and if you're squeamish you should find some-

Breaded Broccoli is one of those delicious "parade" dishes made at the last moment and served hot.

It's nice to sprinkle the Breaded Broccoli with parmesan cheese just before serving.

I
Remember
Pasta

one who loves fishing or who is an expert on cleaning fish to show you how to remove the eyes and the cartilage within the tentacles. The skin must also be removed as much as is humanly possible, for that is where the toughness occurs when cooked.)

3. Once squid is cleaned, the body should be cut into 3/4" wide rings by cutting across the length of the body. Keeping the tentacles as much intact as possible. When all squid is cleaned, cover with ice water in a bowl or store in refrigerator until last 20 minutes of cooking the tomato sauce.

4. Cut garlic into small pieces and return to pot. Combine all ingredients in saucepan, stirring well; bring to boil, reduce heat, and simmer for one hour.

5. Add cleaned squid and simmer 20 minutes. Stir sauce during last 20 minutes.

6. Boil 1 $\frac{1}{2}$ to 2 lb angel hair or thin spaghetti, drain as usual and cover with parmesan cheese and calamari sauce.

7. Garnish with last sprinkle of parmesan cheese and serve immediately.

DEEP-FRIED CALAMARI
Serves 8

This one is a last-minute job.

> 1 $\frac{1}{2}$ lb squid
> 1 $\frac{1}{2}$ C light oil
> 1 C flour for dredging
> salt and pepper

1. Preheat deep fryer to highest setting.
2. Clean squid as described in recipe for Calamari Sauce (pg. 89).

3. Cut squid in 1/2" rings and keep full tentacles intact.
4. Dip squid in flour, coating lightly.
5. In preheated deep fryer, drop in pieces of squid and allow to cook until crisp and golden brown (approximately 2 minutes). Keep oil as hot as possible.
6. Remove from oil and drain on paper towels; salt and pepper immediately and serve.

SMELTS
Serves 8

These funny little fish are a bit of tedious work in that they must be very well rinsed inside and out, and with sharp scissors all tiny fins and the top fin must be clipped away. Because they are tiny, the skeleton and tail are eaten as well. It is a crispy, delightful adventure and rivals all those potato chip commercials that dare you to eat only one! So here goes!

> 2 lb smelts
> 1 C flour for coating
> 3/4 C light oil
> salt and pepper to taste

1. Heat oil in skillet until hot.
2. Once smelts are cleaned and fins clipped off, roll them in a shallow bowl of flour, shaking off excess.
3. Sauté in hot oil until golden brown and crisp on one side. Then, turning only once, cook on second side until well done.
4. Drain on paper towels; salt and pepper to taste and serve hot!

STEAMED KING CRAB LEGS
Serves 8

> 16-20 crab legs
> salt
> water
> 1/2 lb melted butter or margarine
> seafood cocktail sauce (optional)
> 8 nutcrackers

1. Scrub crab legs well and with strong scissors cut at joints into smaller pieces.
2. Boil salted water in pot large enough to hold all the crab when at the fastest boil.
3. Add crab legs and boil until pink.
4. Melt margarine (or butter) and place in 8 small bowls around the table so that each guest has an individual bowl for dipping crab meat.
5. Pass cocktail sauce for those not wishing to dip crabmeat in melted butter.
6. Place a nutcracker at each place as a part of the table setting—to help your guests crack open their treat!

SCAMPI IN GARLIC AND PARSLEY SAUCE
Serves 8-10

> 50 large shrimp, with shells
> 12-16 cloves garlic, sliced lengthwise
> 1/2 C light oil
> 1 stick margarine
> 3/4 C grated parmesan cheese
> 1 C chopped parsley
> 5-6 ice cubes
> coarsely ground pepper

1. Wash shrimp and remove portion of shell up to tail, but leave all of the shell on the tail.
2. Butterfly each shrimp by cutting the under body where the legs are attached almost through to curved edge of the back.
3. Cut from neck to tail from underneath—deeply enough to split open the length of the body and allow you to spread or "butterfly" the two sides.
4. Melt butter, add to oil in large skillet and brown garlic. Reserve.
5. Sauté shrimp in garlic butter, turning quickly until they just turn pink.
6. Sprinkle with chopped parsley and add ice cubes.
7. Cover tightly and reduce heat to simmer for 2-3 minutes.
8. Sprinkle with parmesan and coarse pepper and cover again. Cook for one minute and serve.

CANDIED YAMS
Serves 6-8

> 6 large yams
> 3/4 C dark brown sugar
> 1 stick margarine
> sprinkling of cinnamon, nutmeg, cloves

1. Wash and prick each yam 6 times with a fork. Boil 6 whole, unpeeled yams until fork tender; do not overcook.
2. Remove from water and peel.
3. Slice yams lengthwise in 3/8" slices.
4. Grease a large shallow baking pan.
5. Layer yam slices in baking pan, side by side, in bottom of pan.
6. Dot with margarine and evenly distribute brown sugar over all.
7. Sprinkle all with cinnamon, nutmeg and cloves, using twice the amount of cinnamon to nutmeg and cloves. Be careful not to use too much cloves—it is potent.

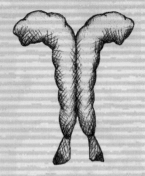

Using ice cubes for steaming the shrimp quickly is an innovation I invented.

8. Add 1/2" water to bottom of pan; cover and seal tightly with aluminum foil.
9. Bake at 350° for 30 to 40 minutes; if possible serve in baking dish.

Optional topping:

> 1 package marshmallows
> > (regular or miniature).

1. Just before serving, cover entire dish of yams with marshmallows and place in broiler just long enough for marshmallows to brown.
2. Be certain each scoop of yams contains a marshmallow.

STUFFED VINEGAR PEPPERS— "THE LONG ONES!"

Serves 6-8

This is a taste treat unique in all the ethnic dishes I've ever sampled. Only my mother knows how she concocted the combinations.

Step One: Pickling the peppers

> 6 sweet green bell peppers, the
> > longest variety available
> 3 qts water
> 1/2 C white vinegar
> 1 bay leaf
> 3 cloves garlic, sliced lengthwise

1. Wash peppers, remove stem, seeds, and ribs from inside. Leave whole.
2. Boil peppers in water with spices just until tender, remove from water and cool.

Step Two: The Stuffing

> 2 1/2 C bread crumbs
> 1/2 C oil
> 1 C honey
> 1/2 C sugar

> 3 anchovy filets
> 1/2 C raisins
> 1/2 C chopped walnuts
> 1 C dried figs
> 2 cloves garlic
> salt to taste

1. Fry breadcrumbs in hot oil.
2. Grind anchovies, raisins, nuts, figs, and garlic together in food processor.
3. Mix all ingredients well and fill whole, boiled peppers.
4. Put in shallow baking dish, dribble with oil and bake at 350° for 1 hour.
5. Place on platter and slice in 1" rounds. May be served hot or cold.

SUGAR COOKIES

Makes 2 dozen cookies

> 2 1/2 C flour
> 1 1/2 t baking powder
> 1 t salt
> 1 t cinnamon
> 1 C sugar
> 3/4 C light oil
> 2 eggs
> 1 t vanilla

1. Sift flour, baking powder, salt, and cinnamon together.
2. Combine sugar and oil and beat in eggs one at a time.
3. Combine egg and flour mixtures and blend well.
4. On a lightly floured breadboard, roll dough to 1/4" thickness and cut forms with shaped cookie cutters.
5. Decorate cookies to suit the occasion— there are endless choices of colored sugar and candy sprinkles for angels, trees,

sleighs, bells, stars, and wreaths.

6. Decorate snowmen with red-hot candies for buttons, and mouth, and chocolate chips for eyes and nose.

7. Once finished, these cookies are baked on a greased cookie sheet for 7 to 10 minutes at 375°. Careful not to over-bake!

APPLECAKE WITH WHIPPED CREAM
Serves 8-10

> butter and flour for pan
> 3 eggs
> 2 C sugar
> 1/2 C vegetable oil
> 3 C flour
> 1 t baking soda
> salt
> 1 t cinnamon
> 3 C peeled and coarsely chopped apples
> 1 C chopped pecans
> 2 t vanilla
> 1/4 lb butter
> 1 C light brown sugar
> 1/2 C milk
> whipped cream

1. Preheat oven to 325°.
2. Butter and flour a 10-inch tube pan.
3. Beat the eggs with the sugar until thick and forms a ribbon when a spoonful is lifted and dribbled to the surface. Add vegetable oil and beat until blended. Stir in flour, soda, 1 t salt, and cinnamon. Blend well.
4. Stir in apples, pecans, and vanilla and mix well. Turn batter into prepared pan. Bake 1 hour and 15 minutes, or

until a knife inserted in center comes out clean.

5. Make topping: Melt butter in a saucepan, add brown sugar, milk, and a pinch of salt and boil for 3 minutes.
6. When cake is done, cool for 5 minutes in pan, then turn out onto serving platter. Prick a number of holes over surface of cake, using a skewer or a toothpick, and while still warm pour topping over cake. Serve with whipped cream.

CARAMALIZED TAPIOCA
Serves 4-6

This was my mother's creation, probably because I hated white tapioca.

> 3 C hot water
> 1/2 C tapioca
> 1 1/2 C brown sugar
> 1/2 t salt
> 1/2 C chopped pecans or walnuts
> 1/2 pt whipped cream
> dash of vanilla
> sprinkling of powdered sugar

1. Boil water, combine with salt and sugar and mix well.
2. Reduce heat to medium flame and add tapioca a small amount at a time, stirring constantly to keep from lumping.
3. Raise heat and stir until tapioca begins to thicken.
4. Remove from heat and add vanilla and nuts; stir together and cool in refrigerator.
5. Serve with whipped cream with vanilla and powdered sugar added to taste.

BLARNEY STONES
Serves 20-22

Aunt Ange devised this tempting sweet and teased anyone to eat just one.

Yellow Cake:

    3 C sifted cake flour
    2 1/2 t baking powder
    1 t salt
    3/4 C soft butter or margarine
    1 1/2 C sugar
    3 eggs
    1 t vanilla
    1 C milk

1. Sift flour with baking powder and salt; set aside.
2. In large bowl of electric mixer, or with whisk, at high speed beat butter, sugar, eggs and vanilla until light and fluffy—about 5 minutes—occasionally scraping side of bowl and guiding mixture into beaters with rubber scraper.
3. At low speed, or with a wooden spoon, beat in flour mixture (in fourths) alternately with milk (in thirds), beginning and ending with flour mixture, and beating only until smooth.
4. Prepare large rectangular cake pan by greasing and coating with flour. A larger pan (9"x 12") will stretch the batter into a 2" high cake and make 2" perfect squares.
5. Pour batter into prepared pan; bake at 350° 30-35 minutes, or until surface springs back when pressed with finger.
6. Cool in pan on cooling rack for 10 minutes; remove from pan and cut into 2" squares; frost as per instructions.

Frosting:

    1/3 C soft butter or margarine
    3 1/2 C sifted confectioners sugar
    3-4 T light cream or milk
    1 1/2 t vanilla

1. In medium bowl, beat butter with sugar, 3 T cream or milk, and vanilla until smooth and fluffy. If frosting is too thick, add milk a little at a time until desired consistency is reached.
2. Spread on all sides and top of cake squares.

For Blarney Stones:

    toasted coconut
    crushed peanuts

1. To toast coconut: Place a single layer of coconut onto a cookie sheet and place in a 325°oven. Watch carefully and stir often with a wooden spoon as the coconut will burn easily. Toast until light brown.
2. Crush skinned peanuts between two sheets of waxed paper with a rolling pin until very fine.
3. When cakes are frosted, roll half of the cake squares in peanuts and the other half in toasted coconut.
4. Place on separate serving plates, or serve as part of cookie tray.

(left to right, seated) My father and me; (standing) my cousin Vince Laraia, his wife, Ruthie, my cousin Marilyn Loraia, and my mom—at the banquet for Carol Lawrence Day

KOLACHES—JAM STARS

Serves 6

My mother stole this recipe from one of her dear Polish pinochle partners.

> 1/2 lb margarine
> 3 oz pkg cream cheese
> 1 egg
> 2 C flour
> 1 t baking powder
> 1 C strawberry jam for filling

1. Preheat oven to 350°.
2. Mix all ingredients in large bowl. Mix well.
3. Roll out on floured bread board. With a rickrack ravioli cutter, cut into 2-2 1/2" squares.
4. Place 1/2 t of jam in center of each square.
5. With same ravi-oli cutter, make a slit from each corner to near the jam center, as per illustra-tion:
6. Pull corner 1a and attach to jelly center; repeat with corners 2a, to stick to jam center, 3a and 4a the same—so you end up with a four-pointed star, or pinwheel cookie with a jelly center all covered and secure in the dough: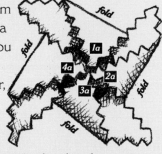
7. Place onto a greased cookie sheet and bake at 350° for 20 minutes.

PRALINE-PUMPKIN PIE

Serves 8

> 9-inch unbaked pie shell
> Cool Whip or whipped cream
> (if desired)

Praline Layer:

> 1/3 C finely ground pecans, firmly packed
> 1/3 C light brown sugar, firmly packed
> 2 T soft butter or margarine

Filling:

> 2 eggs
> 1 C canned pumpkin
> 2/3 C light brown sugar, firmly packed
> 1 T flour
> 1/4 t cloves
> 1/8 t mace
> 1/2 t cinnamon
> 1/2 t ginger
> 1/2 t salt
> 1 C light cream

1. Prepare pie shell; refrigerate until ready to use. Preheat oven to 400°.
2. Make praline layer: Blend all ingredients in small bowl. Press gently onto bottom of pie shell, with back of spoon.
3. Make filling: In medium bowl, with rotary beater, beat eggs until frothy. Add remaining ingredients, in order; then beat only until well mixed. Pour into unbaked pie shell; bake 50 to 55 minutes, or until tip of sharp knife inserted in center comes out clean. Cool thoroughly on wire rack.

You may top the Praline-Pumpkin Pie with whipped cream for a lavish dessert.

Grace Within Our Hearts

THE PREVIOUS CHAPTER IS AN ELABORATE AND YET FITTING tribute to the birth of Christ and the worship of God. It is only from His bountiful blessings that we are fed physically as well as spiritually. And so for my final chapter, I'd like to give thanks for all of His gifts to us.

In my journey to being a born again Christian, and learning the promises and covenants with our Father, I marvel at the miraculous power of prayer, and try to find time throughout the day to consciously dialogue with my God. Certainly, the most easily identified moments are the graces that preface our meals. The best ones are created on the spot. Here's my suggested breakfast opening:

> *Heavenly Father, we praise You and Your merciful grace that gives us a shining new day. Help us to walk strong, work joyfully, and fill the day with steps that fulfill Your plan for us. We give thanks for this food and ask that it fortify us to continue our life in Your light. Amen.*

As for the hectic rush of business and catch-up social luncheons, a simple question like, "Would you mind if we took one minute to ask a blessing before we eat?" is more appreciated than we know. Short and sweet is the formula:

> *Dear Lord, we give You praise and thanks for food and these friends with whom we share it. May it bring strength to our bodies and joy to our souls. Amen.*

And then a thank you to those you are lunching with for the sensitivity to your need for grace is all that's necessary.

Dinner time is really an opportunity for all responsible parents to instill a constant thankfulness for all the Lord's blessings on those who encircle your table. I find the gesture of holding hands sets a peace and calming touch. It allows us a release from the tensions that have invaded our day. Nothing needs to be a sermon. It would be difficult to remain compassionate when a perfectly timed soufflé is sagging into a puddle in the kitchen while grace is being stretched out too long. Prudence and practicality should reign!

> *Dear Lord, we join together in thanksgiving for the bounty of Your blessings. We praise You always, and at the close of this day, we ask Your protection and guidance toward completing the plan You made for each of us so long ago. Amen.*

In concluding this little book, my personal prayer to you as a reader would be to take the precious recipes and make them your own individual messages of caring and understanding and appreciation for all those closest to your heart. Take their hands and work the ingredients into cherished memories they can taste every time they think of you— that's where love abides.

Buon Appetito!